A Group Home for Adolescent Girls: Practice and Research

Joseph L. Taylor
Jerome L. Singer
Harriet Goldstein
Margaret O. Tsaltas
Elaine Kasowski

A PROGRAM OF
THE ASSOCIATION FOR
JEWISH CHILDREN
OF PHILADELPHIA

Child Welfare League
of America, Inc.
67 Irving Place
New York, N.Y.
10003

Book Design by Mary Jaquier O'Sullivan

Acknowledgments

The Association for Jewish Children of Philadelphia expresses its warmest appreciation and gratitude to Lessing and Edith Rosenwald for funding the major research study; to the William Penn Foundation, which financed the Predicted Outcome procedures; and to the Max and Anna Levinson Foundation for meeting the costs of publication. Assistance with statistical analysis from John Herrera and Joshua Auerbach is acknowledged with gratitude.

Contents

The Practice

The Research

Publisher's Preface

A Group Home for Adolescent Girls: Practice and Research is vitally needed, and therefore particularly welcome at a time when the child welfare field is struggling to deal with three wide and urgent trends. One is the flooding into agencies of disorganized, violence-prone, disturbed and often well-nigh uncontrollable adolescents. The second is the emergence of small-group, community-based care in place of the large, isolated institution, on the one hand, and, on the other, traditional foster family care that can neither absorb such difficult children nor, by definition, offer a stable roof over their heads. The third is the demand for accountability laid upon social work, as well as other fields, in a world of limited resources.

Agencies have responded to the first two trends by proliferating a bewildering variety of group homes and residences. In its publications, the Child Welfare League has sought orderly and principled concepts to provide a firm structural base for these settings. In 1977, the League expects to publish a new set of standards for group home care as a full-scale guide to the field. The literature on evaluation and accountability is also proliferating, and is gradually pulling together a set of manageable criteria.

A Group Home for Adolescent Girls: Practice and Research contributes markedly both to the development of one model of group home care and to a methodology for evaluation. Although it originated as a followup study of a group home treatment program at the Association for Jewish Children of Philadelphia, it extends its horizon by presenting a thorough philosophy of care and a detailed description of the setting and its staffing, thus enhancing its value as literature for the field and as a text. Such care comes neither easy nor cheap, but it results in lasting benefits to the children and the community. This is a program guided by disciplined thinking, by a research effort of integrity, and by the devotion and skill of staff members and volunteers at all levels.

The book has the final virtue, dear to a publisher's heart, of being vastly readable and consistently interesting.

Carl Schoenberg
Director of Publications, CWLA

Note to the Reader

At present there are no generally accepted definitions in the field for "group homes" and "group residences." In time the terms applied to different types of group living structures for children will be clarified, but for purposes of this monograph it is necessary to indicate that although the facility described has been known in the community as the Girls' Residence, in concept and structure it has been considered a group home.

Foreword

Adolescents who require treatment through separation from their families are among the most troubled children in any community. Out of compassion for their plight and concern for their future, communities have developed various forms of substitute care, one variety being small-group residential treatment. Thousands of adolescents annually are treated in group homes, and the costs in effort and money are heavy. At present such services are being widely recommended as an alternative to traditional forms of substitute care for older children. But at the same time these programs are being subjected to a great deal of question. Do they accomplish good? Can evidence be furnished that they achieve enough improvement in the social development and emotional well-being of children to justify the heavy investments that are made? Should such placements ever be anything more than a treatment of last resort after prolonged efforts have been made to keep young people in the setting of their own homes?

The outcome of group home treatment—the proof that benefits do result from it—is only one factor in assessing the utility of a service that by definition often deals with adolescents for whom society today can provide no other choice. Nevertheless studies of outcome are needed to document results achieved, and if the study of results can be related to an examination of the processes that produced the results, society is better prepared to make judgments about the effectiveness and improved operation of programs.

The Association for Jewish Children of Philadelphia, a multifunction voluntary children's agency, undertook such an evaluation through an outcome study of all girls (24) who had completed a stay in the Girls' Residence from the date of its opening in August 1959 to December 31, 1969. The subjects were adolescents who entered the program from ages 13 to 15.

In addition to the report of research, this monograph describes in some detail the group home that was studied. Such an account seems useful because the term "group home" is only partly self-defining. To paraphrase William James's observation that an individual has as many different selves as there are persons who recognize him, there are probably as many different types of group homes as there are organizations that operate them. There are differences in the physical settings of these programs, in the components of the treatment program, in the relative importance attached to the components as reflected in the time, effort and money invested in them, and in the "mix" of the components. Thus, research findings must be viewed in the context of the professional practice that produced them.

But beyond that, reports of group home programs are scarce, and the writers felt that such an account would be timely. The objective was to set down in a plain, factual way how the work was done. Perhaps the unending necessity to do something about the daily living habits of deeply troubled children, minute by minute, hour by hour, day by day, fuses theory into an action orientation that ultimately makes it easier to describe what one did than why it was done. Between the concept and the execution is a mass of detail that makes the concept work. This is the area to which the practice portion of this monograph is addressed.

If the tone of this report at times seems rather certain, it is not meant to deny that there are other ways of thinking about rearing adolescents and treating them clinically. The persons who operated this program found early that they could not be helpful to children without a point of view and some convictions about how to treat them. Thus, one had to act as though one knew. In truth, one can only look back upon an involvement in residential treatment with humility, for treatment programs in such a complex endeavor are often as much the product of accident as of design, the accidents being the convergence in a special time and place of particular persons, their ideas, personalities, temperaments and skills; particular funding patterns; and the quality of supports in the community upon which the treatment program depends. In many ways those who fashion residential treatment services are like a broken field runner in football who has an objective but who must thread and improvise his way through unpredictable and shifting obstacles. If the player is both gifted and lucky he will reach the goal.

This program was begun in 1959, when the group home movement was in its infancy. There were few guidelines to the operation of such endeavors. Even in 1976, it was apparent in a national meeting of experts on group care convened by the Child Welfare League of America that the field had more questions than answers. In addition to breaking new ground, the program experienced the impact of profound changes in American society between 1959 and 1969. Just as children need a floor of stable care for their physical and emotional development, their growth socially and morally is facilitated when there is stability in the culture in which they are growing up. But when one undertakes the 24-hour-a-day care of children, one is committed to a journey that must continue to its end, whether or not there are road maps, and even should the road at times disappear.

The Girls' Residence
Association for Jewish Children of Philadelphia

The Authors

Joseph L. Taylor, M.S.W., is Executive Director, Association for Jewish Children of Philadelphia.

Jerome L. Singer, Ph.D., is Professor of Psychology and Director of Clinical Psychology Program, Yale University, New Haven, Connecticut, and the director of this research project. Dr. Singer had the major role in the theoretical development of the research. He devised the procedures and developed the Predicted Outcome phase of the study.

Mrs. Harriet Goldstein, M.S.W., Associate Director, Association for Jewish Children of Philadelphia, was the Director of the Girls' Residence.

Margaret O. Tsaltas, M.D., Chief of Psychiatric Service, Association for Jewish Children of Philadelphia, was the Child Psychiatrist at the Girls' Residence.

Elaine M. Kasowski, Ph.D., Devereux Foundation, Devon, Pennsylvania, implemented the evaluation study. Dr. Kasowski executed most phases of the investigation as part of her doctoral studies at the City University of New York. The reader is referred to her unpublished doctoral dissertation for a full review of the relevant evaluation literature and a detailed, technical description of the procedures she employed in selecting specific criteria for study, developing and adapting scoring manuals and rating scales and conducting interviews with all subjects. The outcome evaluation phase of the present monograph, which included intake and followup evaluations, as well as the two Predicted Outcome ratings, were carried out by a larger number of raters from more varied clinical backgrounds and with somewhat different rating instructions. Some differences will therefore be found between the two studies.

The
Practice

The Group Home Program

Presumably outcome in a residential program results from what is done with and for the children. The character and consequently the performance of a group home are derived from the concepts that guide its operation and from the persons who operate the concepts. We begin, therefore, with a description of the program and its components.

Fortuitously, AJC has been on record over the years in a number of professional publications about key elements in the residential program. These publications provide a record of intentions that predate the completion of the research. The objectives and components of the program can therefore be described by reference to the published material.

THE SPONSORING AGENCY

The Association for Jewish Children, which operates the Girls' Residence, is a voluntary agency that specializes in services to disorganized families and disturbed children in the Jewish community of Greater Philadelphia. Founded in 1855, the agency is a member of the Federation of Jewish Agencies of Philadelphia and a constituent of the United Fund of Greater Philadelphia. Up to 1967, AJC offered placement services only, e.g., foster family care, group home care for adolescents (three units for boys, one for girls), adoption and services to unmarried parents.

1

In 1967 a program was begun to avoid placement by serving placement-potential children in their own homes, and in 1970 a family day care program for children under age 3 and school-age day care programs were inaugurated. During the decade covered by this research, AJC served an annual average of 382 children through in-person contacts, including 33.9 different children per year in the four group homes. The several placement services of the agency were operated through departments containing specialized caseloads. The intake department evaluated all children referred to the agency and, in collaboration with the psychological and psychiatric diagnostic services, assigned families and children to the appropriate service within the agency or to an outside resource. The intake policy for the Girls' Residence was open, candidates being admitted in order of application without regard to diagnosis or other considerations that might affect their impact on the group. Girls were rejected only if they were clearly assaultive, suicidal or so mentally ill as to require immediate hospital care.

Funding for the program came largely through purchase of service on a per diem basis from counties in the Philadelphia area from which AJC accepted children. During the decade studied, the per diem payments ranged from approximately 50% of cost at the beginning to about 80% of cost in 1969. Costs ranged from $4455 per child per year in 1959 to $6943 per child per year in 1969. The difference between the rate and cost was covered by other sources of income, including United Fund money distributed by the Philadelphia Federation of Jewish Agencies.

THE GIRLS' RESIDENCE

The Girls' Residence was opened in August 1959 with a capacity for seven girls. Gula (1) has suggested three types of group homes for adolescents:

1) Adolescents who need a minimum of casework services, but do need a constructive group living experience, with helpful adults, in a community setting. Their parents use casework services. Foster family care is not available.

2) Adolescents who need full casework services, occasional psychiatric consultation, professionally supervised group living, with child care staff collaborating closely with casework staff in a community setting.

3) Children and adolescents who need a maximum of casework service, regular psychiatric help, coordinated with therapeutic group living, but still in a community setting.

The AJC Girls' Residence corresponds to 3) above. It was established in response to the referral of girls aged 13 to 16 who needed treatment through separation in an environment that offered structure and controls in a therapeutically oriented daily living milieu. These were adolescents who could not be contained in foster family homes because of their severe symptomatic behavior and their inability to tolerate close family-type relationships. With few exceptions the girls and their parents have been through many of the family counseling, social service and mental health agencies in the community, and the referral to AJC for placement was invariably seen as a last resort after previous treatment had failed to stabilize the girl in her home and in the community. Many of the girls had prior placements in foster homes, institutions or mental hospitals. A search for impulse gratification dominated these girls. They distrusted parents, parent substitutes, teachers, all authority. Denial of personal responsibility for their problems and projection of blame on others were usual. Disturbances in sleeping, eating and other physiological functioning were common. A hunger for the affection that had been denied them by parents impelled these girls to flights from home, sex experiences and other aberrant behavior that might be rewarded with recognition, but the resentment generated by deprivation drove them to sabotage proffered affection.

The residence is a seven-bedroom, center-hall-entrance house in a stable middle class residential area near the northern city limits, rented for the first 2 years and then purchased by the agency. The decision to operate the program in an agency-owned home was based on the expectation that the agency would thus be in a position to determine what the basic mode of living would be, and that the staff could be held to adapting themselves to the needs of the girls and the group. The home was furnished attractively under a grant from the Merle Sand Foundation. The staff consisted of 1) two child care workers, on duty singly under a schedule that was reduced progressively from 52 hours a week in 1959 to 44 hours a week in 1969, and which required sleep-in during a 5-day tour of duty, followed by 2 days off; 2) a housekeeper on duty from 10 a.m. to 6 p.m. to clean, shop and prepare dinner; 3) an M.S.W. director; 4) an M.S.W. caseworker whose caseload consisted of 14 to 15 children and their parents; 5) a child psychiatrist; 6) a clinical psychologist; and 7) volunteers, assigned on a continuing basis. With but two exceptions for brief periods, all girls attended public school. Among the resources readily available to the agency was a psychiatric hospital for children who had psychotic episodes, became suicidal, etc.

The group home had the same director and the same two child care workers throughout the 10-year period; the child psychiatrist was with the program for 8 of the 10 years; the same caseworker for 4½ years; and the housekeeper for 5 of the 10 years. The executive director of the agency, whose role required contact with the girls during the residence director's vacations and at other times, was with AJC throughout the 10-year period. Thus, there was a great deal of stability in the positions that involved direct contact with the girls, and as a consequence in the orientation to treatment.

The Treatment Orientation and Goals

GENERAL CONSIDERATIONS

This section presents an overview of the treatment orientation and goals. Such generalizations, however, tell no more about the character of a group home treatment program than stage directions tell about the story of a play. The script, in this case the detailed account of operations, tells the real story. Not the concepts alone, but the manner of their execution determines the outcome of ideas. Succeeding sections on the components of the program provide a detailed and operational account of treatment activities.

The treatment orientation of the group home was guided by a clearly articulated point of view. This view has been expressed in publications by Goldstein (2) and Taylor (3). Taylor's view places the agency in the role of extended family, conceptualized as follows:

Practice experience teaches that to help children grow up properly and to treat disturbed children effectively, one needs a point of view that encompasses both purpose and means of achieving purpose. Trying to help deeply troubled families and children without clarity about direction is to frustrate good intentions, for lacking an organized and focused approach, one is afloat without a rudder in a sea of human disintegration.

Given that the families in this program could not provide adequate nurturing experiences for the girls; given the parents' poor potential for resuming effective parenthood of the placed girls; and given the length of time that the girls would remain in residential care, the program had to be concerned with a girl's total living, often until she completed adolescence. In effect, the agency was in the position of rearing the girls, and its services had to reflect that task. This parenting role meant that the program had a moral responsibility for the developmental needs of the girls and therefore was required to do for them everything that a responsible parent would do. This responsibility for the ordinary developmental needs of adolescents coincides with AJC's view that the correct treatment approach to deeply troubled youths rests on intensive supports to their day-to-day development. The dominant service is improved total living, as contrasted to modalities that deal with segments of a person's life such as his psychological transactions. Within this view, the major purpose of "treatment" in the sense of casework counseling or psychotherapy is to enable individuals to cope more effectively with their experiences.

From this view a number of considerations can be derived about practice. Goldstein notes that even the obvious ones relating to physical care, food, clothing, medical care, etc., require more than routine attention (4). Treatment, she writes, begins with creating a secure, stable, accepting home for the girls in which all of their material needs are met unstintingly and with dignity. A pleasant home, ample and tasty food, good and stylish clothing, medical care, and so forth are provided as a matter of course, with no conditions exacted. Such a home for girls whose prior living conditions had been highly unstable, even neglectful, creates a solid floor for the other aspects of the treatment program, and it is a visible, tangible demonstration of caring. As Burmeister notes:

> The very regularity of the routine gives security—the three good meals a day, plus snacks, one's own bed, and (the assurance) that the way things were done yesterday is pretty much the way they will be done today and tomorrow. These many seemingly small and minor things can be counted on absolutely, and this gives support and reassurance. (5)

The further meaning of the parenting role (and in this program the further meaning of the treatment role) obligates the agency to provide all the growth experiences that normal adolescents need, as well as the professional services that disturbed persons need. The growth experiences include education, social relationships, religious education and ego-building experiences. Opportunity is provided freely for music lessons, art lessons, dancing lessons, hobbies, summer camping, volunteer work in hospitals, tutoring in school subjects, concerts, theater, religious training. The value of these experiences is suggested by Eisenberg:

> The sense of self-worth may have its foundation in a feeling of acceptance within the family group, but it is little more than self-deception if it is not based upon mastery of skills and values which enable one to be a contributing member of the group. Mastery is acquired in the schools, in the churches, upon playgrounds, wherever constructive interaction occurs. (6)

This ego-directed help assumes that improving an individual's performance, such as teaching skills in swimming or in school, can produce improvement in attitudes and relationships.

The agency recognized that most of the services to achieve these objectives (or funds to purchase outside services) had to be supplied by AJC, for outside sources could not systematically supply the funds or the opportunities for ego-building experiences, or tutors for youngsters with learning problems, or psychotherapy, etc.

The parenting role requires also that adults have a point of view about right and wrong behavior. As a corollary, if children are to grow up with a sense of purpose, organization and efficiency in dealing with life, they require adults who have a point of view about appropriate behavior. Thus, the treatment orientation upheld values and standards of right and wrong and set forth expectations of the girls. Personality, like a muscle, needs exercise to develop. That is the function of values and standards. Adolescents need to be held responsible for their behavior. They do not escape responsibility on the grounds of being emotionally disturbed or having been mistreated by their parents. Attention also has to be given to how the girls dress, their manners, habits of bathing and cleanliness, their use of foul and abusive language, and how much time they spend on home-work. The parenting role includes knowing who the girl's friends are, where she is and what she does. All members of staff, professional and child care, contribute to this effort through their concern and through serving as models to create new attitudes and images for the girls.

The ultimate purpose of the treatment program was for the girls to develop social competence. As stated by Singer in the proposal for this research, the emphasis of the program is to provide an opportunity for improved social adaptation, for the implementation of daily life habits for practical affairs, educational and vocational growth (7). Group identification and an awareness of community and of the resources available in the society were also stressed. Among other reasons, the goal of social competence was emphasized because with few exceptions it could be anticipated that the girls would have to make a postresidential adjustment on their own.

It was expected that treatment would have to begin on rudimentary levels and that progress would be slow. Goldstein observed in her article:

> The girls had not known most of the minimal physical comforts on even an elementary level. They had not known standards of regularity in eating, bathing or sleep habits. They lacked training in manners and had known few consistent limits. Relationships to adults and peers had been neither stable nor satisfying. We knew and came to accept that we would not make up for all these lacks and deprivations. Rather, we set for ourselves the task of responding to that which was healthy in each girl, that on which she could grow—no matter how limited it was. We refused to become fixed on the emotional pathology, which was so prominent in each child's life, and recognized that her experience at the residence could not overcome all that had preceded admission. We believed that if some growth could be started, some satisfactions achieved, and some beginning made in her understanding of the people and events of the past, the girl could approach adulthood with increased self-assurance and maturity. (8)

CONCEPTS OF ADOLESCENCE

The goal in treatment was constant and unvarying no matter the girl's diagnosis. The objective was to start the girls toward realizing two goals as adults: self-respect and the ability to love. By the mid-20s, it was hoped, they would be able to support themselves at work they enjoyed and be able to look for lasting, mutually satisfying love relationships, close friends, lovers, husbands.

The reason for choosing such long-range goals were threefold:

1) If one can achieve these goals, one will have achieved everything in life that really matters.

2) To deal with an adolescent, one should have a perspective about the purpose of adolescence. Adolescence is a transitory state of turbulence on the way to adulthood. It is characterized by intensity, a burgeoning of the physical, emotional and intellectual functions, and a relative diminution in the powers of judgment. At best, if one works to achieve a healthy adolescence, one may achieve a temporary state of balance. Since the purpose of adolescence is to grow, therapy in adolescence might just as well be directed toward the future in which the growth will come to fruition.

3) The girls were sent to AJC from stress situations and might return to stress situations. Unless their reactions to stress change, the future could be as disordered as the past.

The Personality-Disordered

The majority of girls who come to the group home can be diagnosed as having personality disorders. A few general remarks about these girls may indicate the nature of the treatment problems they presented to all levels of staff.* The presenting

---

* The second largest group were schizophrenic. They are discussed in the section, *The Psychiatric Service,* as part of the approach to indepth treatment.

symptoms usually represent maladroit attempts at instinct gratification. In these girls running away is usually not an act of
adolescent rebellion; it reflects an instinctive urge to find physical
shelter, warmth, sexual satisfaction and self-importance, none of
which can be found properly in their own homes or on the
streets. Aberrant sexual behavior is almost always a search for
the feeling of well-being and self-pride that these girls never
experienced in their early years. These girls were never "daddy's
girls" because their fathers were either absent, preoccupied, or
lacking sensitivity to the needs of preschool girls for a father's
demonstrations of affection. Often they were not "mommy's
girls" either because their mothers were psychotic, absent, rejecting or in competition with their daughters for the father's
attention. Many of the girls were the only children or first born,
and therefore worse off because they received the full brunt of
parental disorder without the comfort and modifying influence
of siblings.

These girls came with serious wounds to primary narcissism
and personality function, and with problems in social functioning
based upon a failure to develop trust in parenting persons,
teachers and authority. The girls presented a wide range of
defense mechanisms, with displacement, rationalization and projection being the most common. They tended to externalize their
problems. For example, a girl would say that she performed
poorly in school because her teacher was inadequate or because
she had no private place to study; or she had few friends because
everyone else had more money and didn't want to bother with
her. Girls would say they slept poorly, ate too much, bit their
nails because other people wanted to hurt them, put them
away or ridicule them. Rarely did a girl come in saying she did
poorly in school because she didn't work, had no friends because
she was unpleasant, had neurotic traits because of personal
conflict.

THE CONCEPT OF DEPRIVATION

The deprivation of girls referred to the program is profound,
and an understanding of its consequences is crucial to managing

the treatment process. Spitz (9) has stressed the effects of maternal deprivation in infancy, Bowlby (10) the relative permanence of these effects in later life, and Anna Freud (11) the desirability of continuity in parenting after an original separation. However, little attention has been paid to the peculiar anguish of placed children forcibly separated from parents who neither can take care of them nor are willing to release them for care by somebody else. In these circumstances, children who are separated past 4 years of age rarely transfer their affiliation from their own parents to substitute parents.

These children remain permanently damaged by maternal deprivation because they remember the difference between their natural parents and substitutes. The memory is kept fresh by visits from at least partly rejecting or incompetent parents. The conflicting desires (to express dependency and to express anger) are acted out on staff and substitute parents until the girl develops enough ego strength to resolve the conflict. This ego strength is achieved by "borrowing" from staff until the girl can manufacture her own through the growth process (not by transferring her identifications directly from natural parents to substitute parents). The girl creates a composite, or mosaic, identity through a series of partial identifications with staff. As her cognitive strength grows, the girl is able to understand her conflicting desires and resolve them with staff help. The girl grows around an unhealed and incurable wound to her ego (the conflict created by separation and the reason for the separation).

Analytic theory suggests that if persons fail to resolve the age-appropriate conflicts in each stage of psychosocial growth, they repeat conflicts until they are resolved or they remain arrested at an immature developmental stage. However, experience with separated children demonstrates that the processes of growth (to learn, to become toilet-trained, to read, develop skills, etc.) go on no matter what happens to the girl, but the conflicts aroused by deprivation remain unsolvable until the girl is helped to face them and has the cognitive ability to understand them. For this a girl has to be intellectually at least 6 or 7 years old and capable of generalizing about parental functions. Everyone concerned with her treatment has to understand the difference between a "reactive neurosis," so to speak, caused by deprivation and a "true neurosis" elaborated within the mostly unconscious life of the child and separated from her awareness. In this regard, Settlage and Furer's remarks about anaclitic depression seem pertinent: "Even though the ego anlage is normal, the lack of mothering results in an investment of primitive ego with unneutralized aggression (12)."

The persisting underlay of resentment may account for the continuing negative transference observable in placed children throughout their stay. The passive-aggressive behavior of the placed child stems from this conflict. To hope to cure this with substitute parenting alone fails to recognize the severity and complexity of the girl's suffering. The constant rescue fantasies of persons trying to help these girls compound the problem, because the girl needs the helping people and tries to respond to their needs, finds this unrewarding and accelerates her passive-aggressiveness because of the disappointment.

THE CONCEPT OF CONFIDENTIALITY

The caseworkers and psychiatrist are not only therapists for the girl. They are also consultants and advisers to the group home program, sharing their knowledge of the girl with each other, the director and the child care staff, to develop understanding of her problems and the approach to treatment. The consultative, advisory function brings the clinical staff directly into the arena of the girl's daily living. Although the caseworker and psychiatrist have no administrative power within the agency, the girls know that the advice given by these persons is often followed. Thus, a caseworker or psychiatrist has real power, leading to conflicts of interest in the dual role of therapist to the often unwilling girl and as consultant or adviser to the program. What are the rights of the dependent person to confidentiality in such situations?

The AJC caseworker and psychiatrist acknowledge to the girls and their parents that they will divulge confidences to the agency administration and in a court of law, if necessary, when the revelations are expected to contribute to the girl's growth and development or her mental health. For example, a parent's statements might be used "against him" in a custody suit, and a girl's confidences could be used "against her" in commitment procedures to a mental hospital, or to warn the group home director of impending unacceptable behavior. The child and parents understand that the psychiatrist and caseworker are possible "adversaries" and do not stand in the same position as a private therapist in a private office. Thus, the girls can choose what they will or will not say. This position does not resolve questions about the ethical conflicts involved, but it does serve agency practice in dealing with complex behavior, often highly uncontrollable, that is dangerous to the girl and to the community. In the final analysis, the girls and their parents must trust the professional's basic decency and sense of propriety that she will not expose any more of their personal lives than is necessary for their proper upbringing. Trust is required, too, of the agency, in deciding whether to accept the therapist's advice without the logical evidence that the psychiatrist might at times wish to withhold. Some part of all therapeutic relationships must eventually be based on mutual trust and goodwill. The conflict-of-interest issue in the residential treatment of emotionally disturbed and mentally ill girls may disguise a dread of taking responsibility for decision making.

The Components of the Treatment Program

The treatment orientation described in the foregoing operated through several major components. Goldstein (13) listed them as follows:

The community setting
The physical setting
The director
The child care staff
The caseworker and the casework service
The supporting services, e.g., psychiatry, clinical and educational psychologists, remedial education, medical care, religious education, volunteer services
The peer group

These components and related theoretical considerations are described in the following.

THE COMMUNITY SETTING

In their study of Bellefaire, Allerhand, Weber and Haug wrote:

Our findings made us realize that an internally oriented approach to the child is insufficient. The community must be brought into the institution; increased social demands on the child through accelerated exposure to community experiences are essential. Exposure to the community increases the demands upon the child to be responsible for his own care. In office-centered interviews, the child sometimes learns to evade the immediate responsibility by talking about the past or the future. In the community, however, the child can be helped as he experiences a crisis. . . . The making of more demands on the child within the living, school and work areas may be the best preparation for his postinstitutional experience. (14)

The community setting for the Girls' Residence was selected as the most appropriate locale for implementing the treatment goals and objectives. This decision reflects the intention that the girls work out their problems while living in the general community, learning to use its resources and learning to make the personal accommodations necessary to become responsible members of society. Such a setting is obviously more congruent with an emphasis on social competence than a setting in the country or on a separate campus within the city. The opportunity to live in a community tells children that although they have problems, they are not completely different from other youngsters. The opportunity to gain experience in living the way most people do—and as these girls ultimately will have to live—is diminished if one is placed in specially structured and protected living arrangements. It is one thing for an adolescent to have a temper tantrum or for a group of adolescents to be boisterous on a secluded campus; it is another for such outbursts to occur on a hot summer night within hearing of the neighbors with windows and doors open. It is one thing for girls to use a campus library, attend campus recreational functions, and attend a campus Sabbath religious service; it is another to use a neighborhood library, belong to a Jewish community center for recreational activities, and attend religious services in a synagogue.

Through living as others typically do, the individual learns to observe city curfew, learns about neighborhood standards of dress and deportment and participates in neighborhood cleanup or fund-raising campaigns. Making friends with other children is more possible by walking to school with a neighboring boy or girl, by having a girl friend to the house for dinner, being invited to stay overnight with a girl friend, playing games in the yard or getting together to listen to records. The children learn that a house has to be painted, lawns have to be cut, snow has to be shoveled, the garbage put out, the door locked at night. They give out treats at Halloween and give tips to delivery boys. They observe that courtesies have to be extended to next door neighbors. They have transactions with the local tailor and grocer. The girls must learn to have good relationships with neighbors and other local people to promote acceptance of the residence. Confidence is acquired in getting around the city on one's own as the girls travel to friends and recreational facilities. In short, the community setting provides practice for living successfully in the community.

There are, of course, some negatives. Responsibility for the safety and protection of the girls rests on the single child care worker who is on duty. A girls' residence attracts the interest of prowlers, perverts and gangs. A good relationship with the local police helps. At many points the code in the community was looser than the code in the residence, e.g., dating behavior, tolerance of minor delinquencies, acceptable standards of performance in the schools. At times the permissiveness or laxness in the community undermined the standards in the residence.

The resources to be found in a community, such as schools and recreation centers, do not exist ready-made for use by a group home program. Because the girls do not want to go to school or use a recreational center, or because they do not know how, or are afraid to try, or will behave in ways that alienate the resources, considerable initiative and effort must go into explaining the group home program and the girls to the other persons and organizations and in building working relationships that obtain and sustain the desired services. As in planting and tending a garden, the community must be prepared and cultivated if it is to flower in behalf of the girls. In addition to interpretative efforts out in the community, school principals, teachers, counselors and personnel from specialist agencies have been invited to the house periodically for lunch and talk.

THE STAFF

The Director

Goldstein's article in 1966 described the role of the director from the inception of the program (15). In the AJC definition of the position, the director was responsible for management of the group home and supervision of the child care staff and caseworker. She occupied a particular role in treatment of the girls, and was the agency representative for the program to the community. The position also carried the authority to cut through differences of opinion among staff and make decisions on whatever level decisions had to be made.

Management of the Group Home

It was the primary objective of the program to provide for the girls an attractive, well maintained, smoothly functioning home. Through such a home the agency conveyed its respect and regard for the girls and suggested a model household for their own use in later life. Achieving that objective required systematization of many ordinary things that go into daily living. Even before the home opened, the director organized a network of suppliers and vendors for food, heating oil, laundry, electrical and plumbing repairs, etc. Standing committees of volunteers were formed under supervision of the director to furnish and refurbish the home throughout the years. The director was responsible for meeting city regulations governing fire, health and safety. Operating the household had to include a fluid division of responsibility with the child care staff and budget control.

Supervision of Child Care Staff

The director was responsible for supervision of the child care staff, the housekeeper and, because her professional background qualified her for the assignment, the caseworker. Thus, it was possible to achieve a high degree of coordination as regards purpose, objectives and methods of implementation among all the staff members most closely related to the daily life of the home. The child care workers, the housekeeper and the caseworker met with the director at least once a week. The supervision provided support for their efforts and technical advice for their work with the girls. In addition to the planned individual supervision, the director was available to all staff daily, informally via personal contact or telephone during or after office hours. This availability was especially important to the child care staff, who generally functioned in relative isolation, particularly in crisis situations, i.e., a girl's illness or acute emotional distress. Because every member of staff became involved in the daily scene, roles tended to blur, and through supervision the director was the person who kept roles straight.

In addition to planned and informal individual contacts, the director met with all staff in a weekly conference. Here the girls were discussed, individually and collectively; significant observations of their behavior were shared, problems that impinged on everyone were discussed and clarified, differences of opinion about treatment approaches were aired and reconciled, a sense of unity was renewed, and mutual support was given. These group sessions provided an opportunity for didactic teaching about normal and deviant adolescent behavior, theories about treatment and the use of oneself.

The Treatment Role

The director's role in treatment began at the intake conference, where the purpose and goals of the admission were clarified. Consideration of each new girl had to be related to her impact on the group, and here the director played a key role in assessing the effects of an admission and in building the necessary supports for it among the other girls. The director also had to understand how a new girl would affect the child care staff, the caseworker, the psychiatrist, the neighbors and the school, and bring these things into the open if they were not recognized by the others. Above all, the director had to insure that the intake conference translated psychodynamic formulations into hard techniques and methods for dealing with the daily life of a girl.

After intake the director had a diversified role in treatment. Often crisis intervention was required.

> The director was called at 11 p.m. Esther, a schizophrenic 16-year old, had "split." She was sitting in the corner of the bedroom and was "spaced out." She was groaning, urinating, and calling for her dead mother. While the child care worker was trying to handle her the other girls had become frightened by her behavior and were running around the house. Some were crying; some were screaming; one was calling her mother on the phone. The director arrived within 15 minutes of the call, telephoned Esther's therapist, held and comforted the girl at his direction until hospitalization could be arranged, while the child care worker rounded up the other girls, fed and reassured them. After Esther's hospitalization, the director returned to the house to speak with the girls about Esther and themselves.

> The child care worker on duty heard from Susan that she was tired of being a runaway after 2 days. She wanted to return but was afraid of the consequences. The child care worker reassured her and said the director would come to get her. The director met Susan in center city and, over coffee, reassured her about her worries and fears. The director held that while her actions were understood, they would not be condoned. There would have to be a consequence, but the caring for her welfare was there.

Sometimes the director met individually with a girl when the child's behavior required that she understand the consequences of her behavior as seen by the ultimate authority in the program.

The director had to be conscious always that she exerted a "treatment" influence on the girls, even by her very presence, in addition to specific therapeutic interventions. Stopping in on a late afternoon or at bedtime would open up conversations about an incident in school or in the house, a dress recently purchased, a news story in which the director's views and values emerged.

Sharing their experiences, attitudes and feelings informally with the director gave the girls an opportunity to think and test themselves out.

The director also served a flexible "linkage" role, taking over, for example, after being informed by the psychiatrist that a therapy session had ended in an explosive mood that could have consequences for the group and the child care staff upon the girl's return to the home, or doing the same upon being informed that a girl had been suspended from school and would be returning to the home in an ugly frame of mind. At such times the director attempted both to help the girl and to ease her impact on the group.

Frequently the director took the girls on outings, formal and informal, sometimes planned, sometimes spontaneous—to a movie, to dinner in a restaurant, to a place of historical or cultural interest. Whatever the event, the purpose was fun, group togetherness and enrichment. Although volunteers were available for many of these events, the director felt it important to be with the girls at times just for fun. Sometimes, troubled behavior that emerged on these outings—a girl's being withdrawn, aggressive or sullen—would be discussed with the girl at an appropriate time later, or described to the caseworker or psychiatrist for use in treatment of the girl.

Illness of child care staff or vacation absences often put the director in a coverage role. This provided additional opportunities for the director to have an impact on the girls in respect to the ordinary and the unusual things that occur in a household and in interpersonal relationships. She would rake leaves with them, assist in cleaning the house, help prepare dinner. Beyond providing coverage essential to the orderly life of the home, these contacts perhaps made the director a real life figure for the girls —she could do, as well as talk or lecture to them about doing.

The Director as Authority

The use of authority is a major problem in group care, both for the children and the adults responsible for their care. Staff may use authority feebly for fear of being disliked by the children, or delay using it, making unnecessarily prolonged efforts to "reach" a child through other means. The combined hostile pressures of an adolescent group may erode a staff member's ability to use authority. The failure to use authority has negative consequences for children because their own distortions are then reinforced by the adult's distortion of his own role. As Mayer said:

> Not having roles can mean only chaos, disorder, and insecurity. Within such chaos the unpredictable, unmanageable aspects of adolescence become even more disrupting and frightening. (16)

Aarons wrote:

> The so-called enlightened parent adheres to a befuddled logic, by which to understand the reasons for a misbehavior warrants a permissive attitude toward it. What is required instead is that the adolescent know that the parent does not sanction it. . . . For the superego to wage a successful struggle against regressive drive forces, parents and surrogates must remain constant and firm in maintaining ego ideals, both by espousal and example. (17)

In the AJC program, the director assumed the superego role. Until a girl could make responsible choices or decisions and could substitute positive for self-defeating behavior, the director intervened to declare and to distinguish between right and wrong, between the permissible and the impermissible. As a result, with many girls whose characteristic mode of behavior was self-destructive acting out, the relationship between the girl and the director was a perpetual struggle.

Authority was needed, too, at times among the staff. Although a team approach is useful and consensus is desirable, there are inevitable differences in a group of professionals and child care staff that stem from personal experiences, personality and training. Yet at many points a clear decision must be made, despite the persistence of differences, about whether certain behavior can be tolerated, whether a girl should change schools, have visits with her parents, be restricted to the house, etc. Consultants can offer opinions, but they do not have to live out the consequences of their opinions. Child care staff can know what is right, but avoid the recognition because they fear living out the decision with the girls. Someone has to make the decisions —based, it is hoped, on all available opinions, views and judgments—and then risk and live out the consequences, no matter what becomes entailed in the way of worry, personal inconvenience or hardship. In the AJC program that person was the director.

The Director as Integrator

Another aspect of the director's role was central on one hand to the freedom, confidence and completeness with which the child care staff, the caseworker and the psychiatrist could perform their individual professional functions, and on the other hand, to the integration of their collaborative efforts. The child care staff, caseworker and psychiatrist felt totally free at all times in their direct relationships with a girl, or in their advice regarding a girl, to do or say what they thought was professionally correct because they had complete confidence that the director would do whatever was needed personally or in the support of other staff to tolerate or handle a girl's reaction. A girl might react by running away, or by violent acting-out behavior, or by extreme upset to the point of needing emergency hospitalization. No matter. The director could be counted upon whatever the time of day and on weekends and holidays to do whatever was necessary. The child care staff, the caseworker and the psychiatrist talked to each other without inhibition by status differences; each said what she thought was professionally correct, in a team conference, a hallway meeting or a telephone conversation, because each had confidence that the director would serve the impartial function either of modifying or reconciling conflicting points of view.

Administrative Responsibilities

The director frequently reported to the board of directors and its committees, to enhance their understanding of the program through case presentations and other information. Since many board members served as volunteers in direct contact with the girls and in the group home, witnessing the needs and the behavior of disturbed adolescents and observing the treatment, the administrative staff had many allies and advocates for proposals that would benefit the program.

Keeping the intake department informed about the occupancy factor was another function of the director. Since a vacant bed meant a loss of income, vacancies had to be anticipated so that referrals would be studied, team decisions made and arrangements with girl and family concluded to forestall financial loss.

The Caseworker and the Casework Service

The caseworker's responsibilities included 1) direct work with the girls, 2) direct service to the parents and relatives, and 3) collaboration with supporting personnel within and outside the agency. As a corollary, the caseworker was the link among the girl, her family, the various components of the group home program, the school and the community. The seven girls in the house constituted 50% of the caseworker's caseload. The caseworker saw each girl at least once a week and many times more often, sometimes in the office, sometimes at the house. Interviews with the parents were held at least once every 2 weeks, again sometimes in the office, sometimes at home. There were four caseworkers during the period covered by this study, all M.S.W.s in social work, all female. Three caseworkers left, for reasons that included pregnancy, marriage and a husband's move to another community. The fourth caseworker has been with the program from 1965 to the present.

Direct Work With the Girls

The caseworker began working with the girl when the intake study was completed and a tentative treatment plan had been formulated in a conference among the intake caseworker, the child psychiatrist, the clinical psychologist, the caseworker and the director. The caseworker then participated with the child care staff in orienting the girl to the home, picked up where intake had left off in obtaining school, medical, dental and other records, helped the girl with the feelings about separation inevitable at this point, and arranged about visits and telephone calls to the parents. The admission experience was always painful for a girl.

It was as if she could not go through the door. She kept on going up the two steps and running back to the car even though we had been to the house three times before, and she knew one of the girls there. We did this together about 10 times and finally, after a burst of tears in the car, she walked into the house.

She looked so small and fragile when I left her. The other girls and Mrs. G. were trying to make her comfortable, but she sat scrunched on the bed against the wall, her brown eyes staring, taking it in. She seemed overwhelmed and said she would eat peas for dinner. She ate peas and chocolate cake for dinner for almost 2 weeks.

Subsequent work with the girl involved attention, in collaboration with child care staff, to daily living activities as an expression of the parenting role. Thus in regard to clothing, the caseworker joined with the girl and child care staff in planning purchases based upon the girl's needs, her ability to take care of her clothing, and her individuality, and decided how the shopping would be done, e.g., by the girl alone or with the assistance of a volunteer. (The basic wardrobe for a girl was determined by the agencywide clothing lists, developed according to age). In medical care, the caseworker implemented the routine notification from the agency medical secretary about health and dental examinations, or requested appointments based upon current problems. If necessary, however, the caseworker's attention went beyond concrete matters to deal with a girl's anxieties about health problems and physical examinations; or her misuse of clothing, either materially or in what it revealed about her through failure to wear attractive clothing or to wear clothing attractively; or her use of the personal allowance (also determined by agencywide, age-appropriate standards)—if the girl squandered it, hoarded it, sought to buy friendship with it, or wished to save it for a goal.

Direct service to the girl included casework treatment of her emotional and behavioral life. Here, four themes were generally apparent: 1) personal adjustment and feelings and attitudes about oneself; 2) peer relationships within the house and in the community; 3) education and vocational goals; and 4) relationship to family. In all areas, although the caseworker was understanding and sympathetic about the girl's troubled past, the focus was on expectations for the present and concerns for the future, revolving around some core concepts: 1) the past cannot be eradicated nor can adequate compensation be found to atone for the past; 2) to dwell on the pathology within oneself can be defeating—the here and now must be used to build positive experiences and satisfactions, link by link; 3) the pain of separation from one's family never stops, and separation's impact is felt in new and different ways as one grows up; 4) although reunion with family may not be possible, ties to them remain important, and should be encouraged and supported; 5) a girl should try to make the most of herself—her health, her appearance, her intellect, her personality, her talents, her skills— since living will always impose expectations and one must be prepared to cope; 6) the caseworker should listen to complaints, grievances, unhappiness, but often may be unable to make changes concerning the rules of the home, the rules in school, betrayal by parents, disappointment in a friend; 7) wherever the girl went, whatever she did, she would find limits and authority and she had to learn to live with them; 8) the caseworker, as another human being, is willing to share with a girl the experiences, the ideas and the values she found important in her own growing up.

There seemed, also, to be themes in terms of time. Generally a girl's first year in the residence went into grieving, working through the separation and groping tentatively for direction and goals. The second year was a time for locating strengths, reinforcing or developing them, shoring up the girl in every way possible. The third year grappled with plans for leaving, fear and anger about it and sometimes regression induced by the prospect of moving out on one's own. A stay beyond 3 years allowed additional time for developing positive experiences and personal strengths.

In her direct work with a girl the caseworker utilized primarily the casework counseling skills of ventilation, confrontation, interpretation, support and education. Family therapy sessions with a girl and her parents were common. Throughout, the caseworker presented unobtrusively a role model of an adequate woman. The caseworker recognized that although staff positions in the group home program were compartmentalized, the girl's life was not, and that the director, child care staff, psychiatrist and caseworker would at times have to talk with a girl about the same things, even in the same way.

Upon the girl's discharge from the residence, the caseworker continued with her for at least a year. The aftercare service was intended to help the girl with problems, either as part of her family, or in independent living that involved work, college or vocational training, managing one's own apartment, etc.

Finally, the caseworker orchestrated the resources and personnel within and outside the agency that were involved in the treatment plan for a girl and her family. Thus, the caseworker arranged the 3-month team review conferences, took the minutes, and made sure there was appropriate followup on all decisions. The caseworker recommended and then arranged for community resources (recreational centers, employment agencies, medical services, psychiatric treatment) for the girl, and her parents and siblings at home. The caseworker was the key person in collaboration with the schools—the conference, the telephone calls, the sharing of information to develop and support plans to keep a girl in school and to make progress educationally.

Casework Service to Parents

A complete helping service was available to parents. The service included counseling on problems of relationship within the family and assistance in coping with other matters that affect family life, such as employment, housing, physical and mental health, money management, school problems, recreation, etc. The general objectives were: 1) to help parents lead satisfying and socially useful lives; 2) to strengthen the parents as husbands and wives, mothers and fathers, to the point where they could resume parenthood of the girl who was in the group home; and 3) to help the girl live successfully with the siblings if there were brothers and sisters at home. A wide range of treatment modalities was used, e.g., individual counseling, couple counseling, family treatment.

Parent involvement was effected from the moment of referral or application. The service was sustained throughout the girl's stay in the residence, and there were no limitations on the availability of the AJC caseworker. An answering service could put parents in touch with their caseworker after 4 p.m. on weekends and holidays. Just before a girl entered the group home the caseworker would escort the parents on a visit to see the group home and meet the adults who would take care of her. For a period thereafter the caseworker related to the parents' guilt or grief at the separation, to ease their feelings about it and to prevent disruption of the placement. In the beginning parents often needed support to sustain the placement if a girl ran away, took flight into illness or did not improve magically. Parents can sabotage the early period of placement if the reactions and maneuvers incident to the separation experience are not dealt with.

Personal and social dysfunction among the parents was high. They were characterized by low income, extreme marital conflict or broken marriages, mental illness and a high degree of incapacity as parents. (Only six girls in the study came from intact homes.) All of the families had had contact with social work and mental health agencies before coming to AJC, the number of contacts ranging up to 13. These prior agency contacts had usually been brief, and a great deal had been expected of the parents in the way of motivation for help and rather quick change through counseling. There seems to have been a reluctance by agencies to become engaged in long-term relationships with chronically dependent and incapable adults.

In practice, the general objectives for parents were individualized in terms of the potential for improvement or change. Some parents were chronically unemployable as a result of mental or physical handicap. Some were not available for long periods because they were in jails or mental hospitals. A few parents abandoned their daughters after the placement by moving to another community. With some parents the goals were no more than to ease their demands on the girl, to help them keep visits responsibly and to prevent them from disrupting the placement. Whenever possible a girl would spend Thanksgiving, Passover, etc., with her family. At the very least, parents were informed about a daughter's health, school progress, dating, vocational plans, etc. Interviews were arranged at the convenience of parents, including night appointments.

The AJC program offered long-term, close supports to parents who had demonstrated over the years that they could not cope effectively for themselves, their spouses or their children, and who had been unable to use conventional counseling or psychotherapy either to stabilize a family situation or to achieve improvement. These families had no close lateral aids. With few exceptions they were estranged from their kinship group and the community. If there were competent relatives, they had become weary over the years of the unending problems. Friendships and other social relationships were minimal. For many of these parents who were on the verge of collapse, AJC offered a coparenting relationship (18). The caseworker or volunteer gave advice on how to clean a house, shop for food, use food stamps and cook meals; went to a school with a mother to talk to a teacher, or to the housing bureau to talk with an official; helped work out recreational, religious, cultural, after-school and weekend experiences for family members; and helped parents gain legal benefits to which they were entitled. The caseworker or a volunteer might provide human contact and stimulation for a lonely, depressed mother. For one mother living alone, who drugged herself to sleep every night and could not waken to get to her job on time, the agency answering service rang at 7 a.m. until the woman answered the phone. On mornings when the mother was too drugged to answer the telephone, the answering service notified the caseworker and she went to the home. Aware that the darkest and loneliest hours are those outside the 9-5 office day and during weekends, and knowing there were no friends or relatives to whom the parents could turn, the caseworker was always available, especially by telephone.

A visiting plan was made for all parents and their daughters. The plan varied according to the relationship, the needs, the ability of parent or child to sustain the plan and the benefits derived from the visits. Visits were important, among other reasons, so that together parents and children could experience the reality of their relationship and thereby neutralize fantasies that could disrupt the placement. For younger girls whose parents lived at some distance or at an address hard or dangerous to reach by public transportation, the agency provided drivers to and fro. Drivers were provided also for parents who were too ill, infirm or confused to manage transportation themselves.

The Child Care Staff

There was less clarity about the role of child care staff in clinical settings during the period covered by this study than there was about the role of a caseworker or a psychiatrist. Even in recent years there has been uncertainty about the role of child care staff in residential treatment. Rozentals et al. noted:

> Till now the worker has been neither fish nor fowl. The worker has been alternately defined by what he was not (i.e., not a therapist, not a doctor, not a teacher, not a policeman, not a parent, etc.) or by what he was in a global sense (i.e., a 24-hour therapist; a doctor, a teacher, a policeman, a parent, etc.). Hence the worker was alternately allowed no responsibility or was charged with total responsibility for a child's care. Both extremes were equally impossible to work from in any systematic way for either worker or child. (19)

Nevertheless, AJC had a point of view about the role and performance of child care staff. The orientation underwent some change from the conception at the time the group home opened in 1959, but evolved rather quickly into a model that was retained throughout the period of this study. In terms of the fourfold classification of Polsky and Claster (20) concerning the child care functions, emphasis was placed on the two functions of monitor and support, as opposed to guide (initiating group

activities with the girls) and integrator (promoting group cohesion). Essentially the group home program subscribed to the
views of Berwald:

> Although the super-intensive, around-the-clock treat-
> ment approach seems impressive, it does not seem to
> allow for other very important needs of the children
> which we believe are met more adequately in a less in-
> tense atmosphere, and by persons who can better estab-
> lish a more nearly homelike setting. These other im-
> portant needs are the development of ego and superego
> beyond the direct influence of treatment. Just as in
> medicine, no therapist cures anyone, but only removes
> that which blocks the innate curative forces within the
> individual. And those curative and developmental forces
> need an environment in which the accent is not on treat-
> ment, but on controls, discipline, standards and protec-
> tion in an atmosphere of empathic understanding and
> affection. (21)

The AJC program did not intend that child care staff treat
children in a psychodynamic sense, nor was emphasis placed on
promoting group activities.

Before further discussing the position of child care worker in
this program, it may be useful to describe in some detail the
two persons employed initially, who remained with the program
during the entire 10-year period. Knowing about them may convey a literal sense of the influences to which the girls were
exposed.

An initial attempt to find a suitable married couple failed
because invariably there were serious lacks in the marriage and
in the personality of at least one spouse in each couple interviewed. Following interviews with 140 applicants, two middle-
aged widows were employed, both high school graduates and
both with experience in group care of children. Both women
were felt to have a caring attitude toward children, a sense of
humor and dignity. They also complemented each other—one
was vivacious, the other more serious. One had a talent for
household management, the other for handling money and bud-
gets. One liked cooking, the other sewing. At the time the group
home was opened, the work week was 52 hours, the women were

on duty singly, they slept in and each had 2 days off a week. The AJC personnel standards and salaries were in the middle range of the national norms at that time.

In addition to the child care staff, a housekeeper was employed 5 days a week, 10 a.m. to 6 p.m., for cleaning, cooking, providing relief time for the child care worker on duty, and providing additional child care coverage when the girls came home from school. Agencywide maintenance personnel took care of repairs. Among themselves the child care staff ordered food and supplies, called in repairmen, cleaned the house, handled petty cash, etc.

To return to Berwald's theme, the child care staff was responsible for maintaining standards of physical care and social conduct through hour-by-hour, day-by-day supervision of daily living. This meant different things for different girls. Some youngsters had to be taught to bathe, brush their teeth, use deodorants. Others had to be taught how to dress and wear makeup without looking on the "make." Some girls would not get to school on time unless awakened. At meal time there was always a girl who had to be reminded to use the utensils instead of her fingers, to speak without cursing and to pass the salt instead of throwing it. The girls were expected to make their beds before leaving for school, clean their rooms and share in the general housecleaning once a week, set and clear tables and clear the dishwasher. Dress habits needed supervision daily, for many girls used clothing to express how they felt about themselves (worthless), and staff would point out that if it did not matter to the girls, it mattered to the people who cared about them. In short, the child care staff had to be aware of, concerned with, and react to a host of details in daily living, in themselves ordinary and even petty, but in the aggregate important because they formed the arena in which the girls could be asked to work out some problems of self-responsibility.

Some of what the child care staff conveyed was by indirection. Their attention to the amenities of a household—books, magazines, flowers, tablecloths—communicated something about style. Observance of Kashruth, lighting Sabbath candles, preparing special foods on holidays communicated a sense of Judaism, its traditions and customs.

Often child care staff had to intervene actively, such as in girl-boy relationships, where they had to balance permissiveness with control. The girls tended to develop friendships with children who truanted from school, used drugs and shoplifted, and with boys who sought them as sexual objects. Staff had to use judgment about permitting or excluding certain children when they came to the house. Judgment also had to be used about when to let the girls work out a house or peer problem themselves and when intervention by an adult was needed. The child care worker was expected to make learning experiences for the girls out of planning a house party—whom to invite, what kind of invitation to send, what to serve, how to divide the work and clean up, what to wear. The staff had to handle illness, real or feigned, on the spot, give practical relief for the physical ailment and the emotional accompaniment, call the doctor, get the girl to a hospital and control the impact of illness on the group. Bedtime for a group of volatile girls often required firmness for those who sought to delay with one more drink of water, one last word to a housemate, one more bid for attention, or sympathy for a girl who found bedtime painful because it left her alone with disturbing thoughts and feelings.

The staff had to deal with hostility when they became the targets for wrath or anxiety displaced from a parent or teacher when things went wrong—a visit that did not go well, a friend who failed to call as promised, a scolding in school. Anger over outside relationships was inevitably displaced on child care staff. Konopka noted:

> Another hard problem is the child's relationship with the parents and relatives he has left outside the institution. . . . The child carries his problems of family relationships with him at all hours of the day. His relationship with his parents may be influencing his relationship with his contemporaries. He may feel he is losing status because somebody has found out that his father is in jail. Or he may live in terror because the others may find out that his mother is in a mental hospital and think he is crazy, too. Such feelings color institutional behavior. (22)

Thus, child care staff coped with the daily life behavior of these adolescents, promoted their physical well-being, held them to standards of personal and social conduct, educated them in self-control to protect them from their own impulses and the aggression of others, assisted the growth of peer relationships—all this mainly through their caring, character and resiliency as persons.

The Psychiatric Service

Structure of the Service

The structure of the psychiatric service has been discussed at length by Taylor (21). This article describes the rationale for an intramural service and its advantages over the use of community clinics to obtain psychotherapy. However, girls who were in therapy with an outside psychiatrist at the time of entering the program remained in treatment with that psychiatrist. Although most of the other girls were treated by the agency (intramural) child psychiatrist, an arrangement was made with just one clinic to supply the treatment for girls when the intramural psychiatrist's hours were filled, and for certain girls whose hostility to the agency (as the instrument of their separation from parents) interfered with a successful transference to the agency psychiatrist.

The Content of the Psychiatric Service

The psychiatric service tells a great deal about the entire program because its particular approach to the understanding and treatment of behavior generated concepts that influenced other aspects of the program and, reciprocally, many mental health ideas that were developed in the other components (casework, milieu, education) were incorporated in the psychiatric practice. Although ancillary to the primary purpose of the residence, the psychiatric service was at times crucial for judgments whether or not to hospitalize a child, for explorations of puzzling behavior, for guidance on techniques in daily care that support growth, and for direct psychic intervention (psychotherapy). The functions of the psychiatrist in this program are discussed under the headings of 1) diagnosis, 2) consultation and 3) psychotherapy.

Diagnosis

As diagnostician the psychiatrist determined, through interviews, when indicated, with the girls, and with the parents and siblings, whether emotional or mental illness existed in family members. Further objectives were to describe the family dynamics and the intrapsychic conflicts of the members; to clarify the stresses that confronted those staff members dealing directly with the girl and her family during the period of the girl's residence, including the day-to-day living problems that the girl presented; and to suggest the techniques of treatment that would help the girl and her family deal with these problems. Interviews were held with girls semiannually to reevaluate their condition.

Consultation

The psychiatrist's initial interview with the girl and other family members was discussed in the intake conference, together with the observations of the intake caseworker, the clinical psychologist and the educational psychologist. The director of the group homes, who up to this point had usually not had a direct contact with the girl, participated in the intake conference, as described earlier. A plan of treatment was formulated by consensus. The plan might include the sequence in which problems were to be treated (school, acting out, resistance to placement, etc.) and the roles of staff.

The consultative function included discussions with social work and child care staff, based on oral or written reports, about the meaning of a girl's behavior, or advice on how to respond to or treat a girl's behavior. The psychiatrist was always available beyond office hours by telephone or for examination of girls on weekends or holidays.

Psychotherapy

Decisions for Referral to Psychotherapy

Girls were referred for psychiatric treatment when the consensus at the intake or review conference determined that specific reasons made psychiatric intervention desirable. Usually the reasons involved symptoms of a mental conflict with unconscious components. Within that framework, the AJC psychiatrist accepted in particular girls who were considered less rewarding candidates for psychotherapy. Referrals were made to outside psychiatrists for the reasons stated previously. From 1965 to 1969 additional treatment hours were available from one community clinic that made a special arrangement to take some of the girls.

Preparation for Psychotherapy

Casework appointments began with intake, but unless a girl entering the home was already in psychotherapy, psychiatric referral was deferred because experience showed that children changed sometimes and either did not need a psychiatrist at all or needed one for a different reason after the first period of adjustment to separation was completed. Usually there was a settling-down period following admission. Some girls, either afraid of new people or relieved to escape family problems, began residence uneventfully. Others carried their rebellious or aggressive behavior into the group home immediately. Whatever the behavior, everyone at first made allowances for her to learn group rules and regulations. Usually the "honeymoon" ended when regulations were imposed without allowance for her being "new" and when expectations for performance in the group home and in school were presented clearly.

A testing period ensued, lasting anywhere up to several years. The girl was not just rebelling against authority. She was not only displacing prior parenting experiences onto present parenting experiences. She was undergoing an ego-identity crisis of allegiance to former ways of being and new environmental demands. This was the beginning of the drawn-out struggle of separation from family allegiance to individualization in the residence. No matter how unhappy she had been at home, there was a sense of loyalty to parents that made the girl resist retraining and reeducation by strangers who had different value systems. This struggle was superimposed upon whatever emotional or mental disorder the girl had and was different from it.

The struggle within herself was most often shown in the girl's negativism and self-destructive behavior. It was as if there were so much guilt in breaking away from the past that the child could resolve it only by harming herself. She refused to do what was expected and when pressed would run away, drink, use drugs, cut school or seek sex. At a strategic point in this ego-identity struggle, formal psychotherapy was begun.

The first step in treatment was to establish a statement of why the girl was seeing the psychiatrist in the first place. Since most of the girls externalized their problems, the therapist had to establish goals for them. The girls could see some use for a social worker (to manipulate the environment on their behalf), but they saw no use for a psychiatrist. Nonetheless, appointments were scheduled on a once-a-week basis and were usually kept because the girl lost her allowance or house privileges if she did not keep them. This technique of starting and maintaining appointments was a subject of concern for houseparents and social workers who believed that coercion should not be a part of psychotherapy. Ideally that was true. But psychotherapy could not begin until a mutual agreement was made between therapist and patient, and one could not reach such an agreement with an absent patient. Next, resistance took the form of refusal to talk and, instead, of bringing books to read, and sometimes cosmetics, nail polish and other beauty accoutrements to pass the time. The girls believed that "the silent treatment" would make the psychiatrist give up. This behavior was treated like the behavior of younger children playing with toys in the office; e.g., play therapy techniques were used and interpretations made of their defensive behavior.

At some point the psychiatrist explained the principles of psychotherapy and the ideas governing interpretation of the unconscious. With the lecture went the thought that it was the girls' own associations and behavior interpretations that were helpful, not the therapist's.

More traditional psychotherapy is concerned with the past and how one's reactions to people of the past determine reactions to people of the present. Growth therapy looks to the hope of a better future as a means of motivating change, and toward developing approaches that then become habits and eventually become personality traits that develop stronger and more socially acceptable people.

The past was not neglected. It had to be referred to, at times to be abreacted. But for most of these girls dwelling on the past was a dead end of despair. Thus a girl accustomed to infantile maneuvers in dealing with a psychic mother was more easily helped by comments on her current inappropriate use of such behavior with child care and other staff than she was by being asked to review the memories of her mother's bizarre behavior. The personality-disordered girl tries to relate to people in the present with techniques left over from years of dealing at an arrested level of development with members of her disordered family. The responses of staff persons must withstand her maneuvers and negativism. By concentrating on the girls' interaction with significant staff persons, the psychiatrist encouraged growth by identification with these persons, the girl arriving at a definition of self that included aspects of all the persons who have given her care.

At this point where there was some positive feedback on her behavior and intensification of internal conflict, the personality-disordered girl was ready for psychotherapy.

The Schizophrenic

Since psychiatrists are known to vary widely in diagnosing schizophrenia, it is relevant to note that the AJC psychiatrist's diagnoses of these girls were always supported by the evaluations of the agency's clinical psychologist. The histories of two girls with chronic schizophrenic reaction revealed possibilities of LSD toxicity and/or hypothyroidism as possible etiological factors.

The others were first-time acute schizophrenic reactions, known as a group to have 50% remission.

The treatment of the schizophrenic girls was based upon the psychiatrist's bias in the direction of those who see a possible genetic, neurophysiological disturbance as the basis for the thought disorder in the schizophrenic. Kety (24), Schildkraut (25), Lucas (26), Rutter (27) and DeJong (28) have shown that the symptomatology of schizophrenia may have many causes, including the biochemical. Kety, Rosenthal and Wender (29) and Kallman (30) have indicated a significant genetic factor. Cornelison and Lidtz (31) emphasized family factors in the development of psychosis. Bender, who has done the most complete and extensive followup studies of schizophrenic children, emphasized developmental lags (32). Clinically the therapist is faced with what may be considered a "handicapped" person with developmental arrests, particularly in the perceptual and cognitive areas. These arrests result in maladaptive behavior that causes other persons to reject the patient, who then withdraws. The combination of the maladaptive behavior and withdrawal results in the schizophrenic life style described by Laing (33) and others. Since the progression begins with developmental disorders in perception and cognition, the AJC treatment is directed to these disorders.

The defenses of these adolescent schizophrenics were often compulsive-obsessive. They ruminated about the limits of reality and were obsessed with fears of nonbeing, antimatter, the meaning of words. These obsessive "abstractionists" were better defended than the manneristic, ritualistic, blocked, ambivalent, perseverative girls whose thoughts were so fragmented that guessing at the associations was like finding one's size dress in a rummage sale.

The objective with these girls was to relate one of their obsessions or associations to a socially acceptable vocation or to widely admired productions, such as a book, painting or achievement. In science the questions of the nature of reality are substantive and can be subjected to logical examination. The scattered thoughts and obsessive ruminations of the sick adolescent can be demonstrated to the patient to be related, albeit peripherally, to the thoughts of eminent scientists. The schizophrenics often verbalize their problems in terms of speculations about external reality (such as the nature of elements of crystal formations). The fact that humans can think about the same things forms a link between the psychotic and the philosopher, the artist and the theoretical psychiatrist. Such a distant link may be as much intimacy as the schizophrenic cares to have, but it does permit her to study and to learn intellectually. The intuitive, paralogical reasoning often elaborated by fantasies gradually may be reserved for private thinking, diary keeping, story writing, picture painting and all the other areas (homemaking and child rearing), where this kind of thinking is socially accepted.

This treatment involves teaching facts and ideas. A girl might need to know why the horizon curves, and that although one can visually approximate one's finger to a star, one cannot touch that star. The parameters of reality (both in substance and in theory) have to be explained as one would explain to a very much younger person. Defining substantive and theoretical reality is genuinely useful to these patients because they simply do not know some basic facts and beliefs most people take for granted.

Countertransference in prolonged periods of therapy of this type is prominent in feelings of self-doubt, impatience and near despair. It is like trying to teach the aphasic to converse, or like trying to teach the born-blind to conceptualize color. It is an intensely intellectual exchange, harnessed to an intensely emotional drive to communicate the idea of the thought disorder that is the patient's fundamental trouble. If the girl can truly conceptualize the difference between logical and paralogical thought, she obtains an insight into her problems that permits growth on her own. However, the process of communicating this idea is tedious, time-consuming and often frustrating.

Classically the thought disorder of the schizophrenic is not only one of the necessary criteria for diagnosing the illness, but has also been considered important in the patient's communication problems. Other psychiatrists have treated schizophrenics by dealing with the working through of affective problems in terms of the patients' faulty symbolizing. The process that has been described here is related but simpler.

Group Therapy

The psychiatrist formed therapy groups at times, e.g., when a crisis affected all the girls, when the same issue occurred in the treatment of a number of the girls, when the group had a common reaction to behavior of others, or when it was felt that group treatment would support the individual approach.

Other Staff

A Ph.D.-level clinical psychologist made a psychodiagnostic examination of every girl prior to her entrance into the group home. The standard test battery included the Wechsler-Bellevue Intelligence Scale, Rorschach, Bender Gestalt and Draw a Person. Annually thereafter a psychodiagnostic examination was given to obtain objective evidence concerning the course of a girl's personality and behavior. The psychologist also administered educational achievement tests. (See section on Educational Program.)

The medical service was supervised by a medical director who functioned agencywide. One physician was appointed to serve the girls in the house much as a doctor would serve a family. A panel of physicians in all medical specialties, selected by the medical director to serve agencywide, was available to the house doctor. The medical director, the house physician and the specialists rendered their services without charge to the agency. At times there were costs for laboratory work and material. A nearby hospital, the Albert Einstein Medical Center, Northern Division, a member of the Federation of Jewish Agencies, provided complete medical and dental services, including orthodontia, on the basis of a formal agreement. A psychiatric hospital, the Philadelphia Psychiatric Center, also a member of the Federation of Jewish Agencies, provided emergency or planned hospitalization for girls who needed such care during their stay in the residence, based simply on the AJC psychiatrist's opinion that hospitalization was needed.

Communication Among Staff Members

The individual roles and role performance in a residential treatment endeavor must obviously be integrated into a common purpose and approach if the separate pieces are to contribute to the benefit from each other. Communication, the medium for integration, took several forms. Each member of the intake team wrote a record of his observations, and out of the intake conference came a written initial treatment plan. The child care workers kept a daily log of the events and interaction in the house, the caseworker wrote a summary case record every 3 months and the psychiatrist and psychologist wrote detailed reports every time they examined a girl. These records were shared freely. Informal communication through hallway conferences, dropping into a team member's office, etc., was common.

A child care worker would telephone the psychiatrist if there were something significant about a girl's behavior just prior to her therapy session, and the psychiatrist would phone a member of staff to prepare her for a girl's reaction after therapy. The residence team met 6 weeks after a girl's admission and every 3 months thereafter to evaluate a girl's adjustment. School counselors, parents, relatives and other persons related significantly to a girl's life at times joined the staff team.

THE EDUCATIONAL PROGRAM

Taylor's (34) publication stated the program's views on education of the girls as follows.

Education occupies a central place in the residence program because the consequences of learning failure are fateful. A girl spends 6 hours a day in school, spends (or should spend) time after school on homework and, apart from these defined responsibilities, has school on her mind many other hours during the day. If such a large portion of a girl's total experience is unhappy and troubled, much of her life is filled with defeat. The consequences of school failure affect the future in terms of what it is possible for a person to achieve occupationally, in earnings and in social status. Reversing the cycle of school failure is therapy in itself and a source for strengthening interest and motivation. True, education must be coordinated with other services in the residential program. All of the available daily living and professional supports must be invoked to enrich the milieu. There is much to be said about the anxiety that disturbed children bring to learning, the diagnostic problems associated with physical incapacities affecting the ability to learn, the reciprocal relationships among emotional and cognitive processes and the relationship between remedial activities and the overall operation of residential care. An effective program must deal skillfully with these clinical factors. But after these conditions are met there must be an investment in the educational experience itself that does justice to its importance. Residential care must accord this major task of adolescence the highest of priorities, and support it with the services that will enable each person to realize her potential.

Specific Inputs

Achievement Testing

The inputs begin with knowing exactly what educational problems the girl has. Since 1963 the AJC psychologist has given a battery of achievement tests (tests that compare a child's learning with that of children her own age or grade level in the general population) to every girl who was having school difficulties and to every girl who, though receiving passing grades, was performing below her intellectual potential. It is one thing to know that a seventh grader is having trouble in reading. It is quite another to know that she reads on a second-grade level.

Attitudes of Staff

Staff was instructed to be somewhat tough-minded in their expectations of the girls, because the residence program assumed that the educational experience could be approached as a task without waiting for personality and behavioral changes to be achieved through counseling or psychotherapy or other aspects of the program. The level of expectation had to be individualized for each girl in relation to her emotional-cognitive development. True, as disturbed children they needed psychotherapeutic aids to help them make maximum use of education. But these aids were given in the context of firm expectations that a girl would apply herself to the degree that could realistically be expected of her. Everyone on staff had to think that way—the director, child care staff, caseworker and psychiatrist—and the matter of attitudes was part of inservice training. For example, the training for child care staff included lectures by agency persons and outside experts on such subjects as "The Homework Hour," "How the Tutor Tutors" and "Can Disturbed Children Be Expected to Learn?"

Treatment for some girls required that the paths of evasion and denial of their school problems be blocked. Thus, the director would go to the house at 7 a.m. to rout a reluctant girl out of bed if the child care staff could not get her out unaided; would drive the girl to school for days or weeks if necessary to thwart truancy; telephone the school counselor by prearrangement later in the morning to verify that the girl was still in classes; go looking for her in her favorite haunts if she was reported missing, and escort her back to school.

Study Time

Girls could study when they wished, but there was a structured study time in the house Mondays through Thursdays from 6:30 to 8:30 p.m. Radio and TV were permitted if played quietly. Girls who could not use the time constructively if left alone in their rooms received the attention of the child care staff.

Tutoring

From 1959 to 1966, the tutors, generally school teachers, were employed on an hourly basis as required for given girls. From 1966 on the tutors were volunteers, all ex-teachers with a college background in education, or college students. After being assigned to a girl, the tutor was briefed about the school problem by the psychologist and was informed by the caseworker about the child's personality and behavior. Tutors submitted a weekly report on a standardized form about the sessions with the girl. The tutor and the psychologist met regularly to assess the girl's progress. The tutor and the caseworker met as necessary to discuss the girl's use of tutoring and her behavior with the tutor. There was no time limit on tutoring, and the girls could have remedial help in more than one subject.

School Collaboration

Since 1965 AJC has had a special ungraded class on agency premises for boys of junior high school age. The Philadelphia school system provided the teacher and equipment. However, all but two girls were able to attend public school because of the excellent cooperation given by school personnel. The other two, for brief periods, attended a school that was operated by a mental hospital. Without the extraordinary help given by teachers, counselors and administrators it would have been impossible for many of the girls to remain in public school. School personnel became extensions of the group home staff. Case information was shared freely and the caseworker was in touch, sometimes daily, about the girls. Girls who had been expelled for disciplinary reasons or suspended as uneducable before coming to the residence were taken back in school on the knowledge that AJC would be helping them. From the early 1960s on AJC had an annual luncheon for the 40 to 50 school counselors who worked with the residence children and other children in the agency, to thank them and to bring them up to date on developments within the organization.

Evaluation

Beginning in 1963, diagnostic achievement tests were administered to the girls at the end of the school year to obtain objective information about their progress. Passing report cards and promotion to the next grade were not necessarily accepted as reliable indicators of progress, since some students are promoted for reasons other than merit. The test readministrations also helped to shape educational goals for the following year. The post-tutoring analyses covered the correspondence among intelligence and achievement retests, percentage of girls who showed improved school grades, etc.

There was no single measure of success. Evaluation had to consider the type of progress represented by movement from refusal to attend school to attending school regularly; or movement to making a genuine effort with homework. The time period within which to evaluate results had to be flexible because significant deficits are not overcome quickly, and the desired improvement generally came after long periods that evoked doubt and even discouragement.

Vocational Guidance

Career counseling to identify fields of interest and capability was provided for all girls through an outside specialist agency. AJC's conception of its responsibility for the developmental needs of the girls included locating and obtaining scholarships for college or vocational education (often with the assistance of members of the board of directors), or assisting financially from agency earmarked funds. This responsibility was assumed because the girls' families were not able to help them and because vocational preparation is so important. Most of the girls who went to college became independent of agency financial help by the end of their junior year, through a combination of scholarships, work and loans, despite knowing that AJC would have continued to help.

THE VOLUNTEER PROGRAM

There are many tasks in the AJC conception of treatment that do not require professional education and that can be performed by properly selected and trained lay persons who work under the direction of a social worker. From the opening of the Girls' Residence in 1959, volunteers from the board of directors were used to provide concrete services and relationships for the girls. It was these volunteers who searched for and located the house that serves as the group home. A real estate man and an attorney handled the purchase and the zoning application. In consultation with staff a group of women volunteers shopped for the furniture, accepted deliveries at the residence, supervised the painting and decorated the home.

About a year after the Girls' Residence opened, the staff, having by that time lived through a substantial experience with the girls, reviewed where volunteers could serve. Several areas stood out. In addition to being separated from their families, the girls had few relationships with other people. Some girls were doing poorly in school, performing in math and in reading on second-grade and third-grade levels. Shopping for clothing was time consuming because the girls needed to visit different stores, learn about quality and price and make appropriate choices. Some girls needed an adult to help them select an attractive hair style in a beauty shop. If a child care worker were to do these things for and with the girls no one would be left with the group. Finally, the girls needed many types of growth experiences that would stimulate interests, add to their knowledge of the community and the world, uncover talents and develop skills. Staff concluded that volunteers could become valuable assistants in providing the needed personnel.

Six women members of the agency's board of directors, aged 35 to 45, well educated, middle class, were invited to help meet the girls' needs. The women felt warm toward the girls, they became committed to the residence program and they worked with zest. The volunteers recognized, too, that although they would be giving of themselves extensively, they might receive little in the way of gratitude from the girls. This volunteer group became part of the group home "family," and during the 10-year period rarely did a volunteer drop out.

The same six women performed a variety of functions. They served as Big Sisters. They worked with the director in meeting the recreational needs of the girls on a group basis, taking them on trips to New York, to the Pennsylvania Dutch country, to concerts and athletic events. Several of the volunteers with a background in education served as tutors. At Confirmation the volunteers shopped with the girls for their dresses and arranged a post-Confirmation party in the synagogue. Volunteers were encouraged to invite girls to a volunteer's home for Friday night and holiday dinners, sometimes followed by attendance at a synagogue service. Periodically volunteers price-shopped in stores to bring the agency clothing list up to date, and took the girls shopping for clothes. One volunteer developed a Great Books discussion group that lasted 4 years.

Volunteers thus added another dimension to the concept of extended family. The contacts with volunteers permitted the girls to see how middle class people live, brought the girls somewhat into the mainstream of community life, presented a variety of role and family models (wife-mother, husband-father, friend), and provided experiences that broadened the girls culturally. Children need ordinary experiences with lay people, as well as relationships and services from professionals. This compensates somewhat for the absence of a child's kinship group and enriches life with the warmth, color and sense of belonging that come from the extended family.

After 1966 the group home volunteer service benefited from an enrichment and further systematization of the agencywide volunteer service, as described by Goldstein (35). At that time the volunteer program came under the direction of a professional who recruits, interviews and selects volunteers, determines their specialty within the agency, assigns them to specific departments or services that need their skills, develops orientation and training and serves as liaison to agency departments following a volunteer's assignment.

THE RELIGIOUS PROGRAM

Rarely did the family of a girl belong to a synagogue or to a Jewish fraternal or social organization. Usually there was little of a Jewish character in the home life of these families. As for the girls themselves, none had a Jewish education or was a member of a Jewish youth group before coming to the group home. The families were estranged and isolated from the general community, and were isolated from the Jewish community as well. As a result, the girls had no opportunity to learn about the religion into which they were born and to acquire a sense of religious or ethnic identity. A child's sense of personal identity is built of many strands. Her religion and her ethnicity are among them. As part of its parenting responsibility to the girls and to provide another building block for personal identity, the group home created a Jewish atmosphere and expected the girls to participate in educational activities to learn about their religion and their culture.

The religious program developed gradually during the decade, but from the beginning specific practices included observance of the dietary laws; synagogue attendance at major Jewish holidays; study for Confirmation at age 16; appropriate in-house parties and decorations. The girls were taught Sabbath and holiday rituals and the preparation of Jewish ethnic foods. They were encouraged to attend, and were transported, when necessary, to special synagogue events such as religious festivals and rock services. Information was disseminated about Jewish cultural events throughout the city.

A rabbi had been part of the program on a voluntary basis since its inception. He was consultant to staff on questions, issues or problems concerning Jewishness in the education and the living of children and in the management of each group home as a Jewish home. There were lectures, seminars and workshops for casework and child care staff, as well as in-house programming of discussion groups on Jewish values, ethnics, customs, ritual and history, including the current scene in Israel. The rabbi's synagogue served as the institutional base for the religious program. Volunteers were encouraged to invite girls to their homes for Friday Sabbath dinner and on Jewish holidays.

THE GROUP

Mayer noted that the group experience in a residential facility offers a) pleasure experiences within a basically painful structure, b) manageable and common experiences, c) identification with society through the medium of identification with peers, and d) voluntarism within a compulsory system (36). Wong (37) described the mechanisms of the ego in adolescents as follows:

> . . . Devaluation of the parents ("old man" and "old lady")
> . . . Displacement of libido from parents to peers and parent substitutes
> . . . Reversal of affect (love to hatred, dependence to defiance)
> . . . Possible projection of hatred (paranoia) or turning against the self (depression) (blaming others or blaming self)
> . . . Withdrawal of libido to the self, e.g., narcissism, grandiose beliefs, hypochondriasis, etc. (the mirror as the teenager's best friend)
> . . . Regression, sometimes to primitive ego states, perhaps a pathological withdrawal from reality, often to just childish behavior
> . . . Denial of affect (a denial of shame, guilt, anxiety, and panic, resulting in a "cool" orientation)
> . . . Repression of affect (dangerous emotions bottled up until they can be safely displaced, if at all, sometimes resulting in a sudden, inappropriate pouring out of feelings).

Much of what took place in the group of girls can be understood in terms of Mayer and Wong.

The girls shared several experiences that made for a common bond. Each was separated from her family without choice. Each had to deal with attitudes and feelings about parents. Each was dependent upon the agency to fill her personal and nurturant needs. The need to live within the degree of structure imposed by the residence was novel for all. They also had in common the struggle with adolescent growth, e.g., sexuality, identity. The future—what would become of them, what direction and goals would they find—was a source of anxiety for every girl. This common ground provided the basis for group processes and group activities on two levels, one related to initiatives from the staff, the second to initiatives from the girls themselves. Shifts in population, however, because of admissions and discharges, did not always permit a stable population for the group and the severe acting-out behavior of the girls during certain periods was disruptive. Peer group influences from outside the house—a school clique, a neighborhood group, or the presence of friends and acquaintances in the home itself—would exert pulls that kept the house group from becoming a fixed or even predictable entity.

One learns quickly in starting a residential program that the group is a powerful force that must be addressed consciously if its actions are not to become counterproductive. Staff's utilization of the group took several forms. Trips, outings and parties were organized, including efforts to involve the girls in planning. A consensus from the girls was sought on choice of colors for bedrooms, selecting curtains, bedspreads. Group sessions were conducted by the director once a week. Sometimes the girls would ask for a house meeting to clear the air. In these meetings the girls discussed the house rules, and wrote and rewrote them. The talk was often about placement and the separation experience and about typical concerns of adolescence, including struggles with adults and themselves. Dating behavior and theft of each other's boyfriends was a recurrent theme. Notes kept by the girls at some of these meetings are illustrative.

> We talked about a new girl who is coming into the residence. She will be sleeping in the front room. She is 15½ years old. She is a refugee from Cuba, and she knows some English.

> We talked about general problems and decided we'd like to talk about the following in some of the next meetings: taking things that do not belong to us; the housekeeper; usage and consideration of the telephone; consideration for others; loud voices and cursing; smoking rules; relatives, male visitors; television privileges; relatives and parents; dating; respect for adults; our future; sex; value of money; home chores; house key privileges.

> We agreed to talk about taking things that do not belong to us and consideration for others at the next meeting. (December 21, 1961)

We take things that do not belong to us because of jealousy and feeling insecure. We have disagreements with each other. We take things because we do not have the particular item. Sometimes we do it for spite. Sometimes, if we suspect someone took something from us, we do the same to them.

We decided if we're suspicious of someone, not to talk to others about it. We must not become excited or scream because that will cause fear and the suspect will not admit or return the item. Try not to make the involved feel low or unwanted but instead try to talk to her with maturity. No one in the house is a real thief. I know we talked about lots more, but I can't remember. (January 11, 1962)

"Passover—The Festival of Freedom" was discussed and the significance of the holiday. This got us into remembering our family and questions about marriage. We talked about the cycle of love, marriage and divorce. Is that the style—why do marriages fail and if it doesn't work, will we divorce? E. thought it was a 50-50 give and take. How do you look at marriage and when . . . when education is completed? . . . when we can handle problems? . . . when we are mature? What is maturity? We talked about age maturity and feelings and about physical and mental maturity. Some of us talked about control of ourselves and taking life for what it is worth. E., D. and G. especially talked about their family experiences and background. D. and C. talked of their parents' situation, especially their unsatisfactory marriages, and this colored their attitudes. M. said that there wasn't much pleasure or enjoyment in life, and it was all pretty grim for her. We tried to show her that there would be satisfaction in marriage and with maturity. (April 12, 1962)

On the whole, however, although the girls could be mobilized for specific, short-term tasks, they were not interested in staff-initiated activities. The girls would participate individually in community-based programs for group dancing or calisthenics, but were not interested when specialists in these areas were brought into the residence. This may have been due to the quality of the leadership, the nature of the group at the time, or failure to appreciate the group's interests. The most successful activities were a Great Books Discussion Club, and religious and nonreligious activities developed by a young rabbi. The rabbi's program lasted about 5 years. These two favorable experiences seemed directly related to the deeply caring, sensitive qualities of the adult leaders.

The group initiatives from the girls themselves were important to them. The group was often in action behind closed doors. One girl's pleasure or a tragedy might bring them together spontaneously to talk it over. They would comfort one another over transgressions or poor school grades. The girls had a network that organized celebrations for a graduation, a birthday, a holiday. But love and hate relationships fluctuated. The girl reviled today was adored tomorrow. They could be calculating in vying for positions of leadership. Sometimes their anger at one another was enormous, the threats and language hair-raising. An adult intervened when physical harm or other extreme acting-out behavior was in prospect, but usually staff recognized that the girls needed to be left alone to work things out.

THE "MIX"

The separate components of the group home program contributed to the girls' growth and development. The components also combined to create an influence toward treatment in which the whole meant something more than its parts. Intended or not, the activity of the director, the casework, the psychiatric service, the peer group, the dynamics provided by the community setting, and so forth, affected each other and interacted to form a total influence. In education, for example, to what extent might improvement come from the remedial program, or casework counseling, or psychotherapy, or the improved daily living? The reciprocal influences among these factors make it difficult, if not impossible, to separate out the impact of any single factor. The group home program operated on the assumption that all of the components combined to constitute therapeutic intervention, and that they had an interlocking and reinforcing effect. Thus, a "mix" of some kind took place—as with light, made up of different rays that fuse into one visible beam unlike any in its spectrum, or like water, which combines into something different from its ingredients. The mix is thought to include the following:

1) The constellation of efforts and services offered a deeply caring environment. The clinical services and the social services were, to be sure, all directed to creating a better life for the girls, but caring is what translated the abstractions of "program" into a meaningful experience between human beings. Caring is an invisible cement that holds two persons together, usually out of a mutual wish, but if necessary out of the unfailing determination on the part of one to help another. It says: "You are important to me. I want good things for you, and I will do everything I can to bring that about." Caring is unspectacular in itself, but few things for good among human beings are accomplished without it. Caring means giving of oneself even when the response and visible progress of children are discouraging, as they usually are in residential treatment. Caring ignores personal inconvenience, as when the director or caseworker would spend a whole night looking for a runaway girl; or when child care staff would sit up all night with a girl in acute distress; or in the enormous amounts of personal time given by professional and child care staff when the girls wanted them or needed them, for celebrations such as birthdays and school graduation, or for a crisis in school or in court.

2) The confluence of forces within the total program offered a daily living environment that provided nourishment for personal growth and development. The nourishment took the form of caring, encouragement, expectation, direction, pressure and practical assistance toward self-improvement. The atmosphere was affirmative and forward looking, in which doing something about the present was more important than reconstructing the past and in which living had to prepare for a future that exacted its requirements with each passing second, intellectually, emotionally and socially. The knowledge base and techniques of the

social sciences are not yet precise enough to select and arrange the components of experience that will guarantee growth, but there is agreement that certain preconditions (those already described) create the climate for growth.

3) The total environment contained a wide variety of potentially beneficial influences. If casework did not make a therapeutic impact, the psychiatrist might, or the peer group, or a volunteer, or a teacher in school. No one treatment component had to carry the sole or major responsibility for delivering help. No one component was judged a failure if it did not achieve a visible therapeutic effect. It was anticipated that the girls differed in their needs and their readiness to use help. It was expected that the girls would accept some of the aids and experiences offered them and reject others. It was accepted that the service that sparked one girl might be inert with another.

4) There is one component of the program that is difficult to describe, yet it was crucial to the entire operation. This component provided an emotional force that touched and colored everything else. This was the *intensity* of the involvement of the director. The director's commitment created a standard of expectation about the quality of the home at all times and how it met the girl's physical and emotional needs; about the performance of staff, what kinds of persons were hired, what they would give of themselves, attempt and endure in their relationships with the girls; and finally for literally breathing the will into resistant girls to make something of themselves. On one hand, there could be no lagging or flagging of effort because of the director's expectations. On the other hand, there could be no obstacle to risking whatever a staff member thought was the professionally correct thing to do for, with or about a girl, because the director could be counted upon to pick up the pieces, handle the problems and provide the necessary supports with the girls, with the staff, with the schools, with the neighborhood and with the rest of the community.

Among other things this high intensity made for an availability of the director's concerns, time, energy and problem-solving skills that created bridges among the separate people in the program, who necessarily functioned in relative isolation from each other and who inevitably, by their actions, created consequences for the girls and for other members of the staff.

The quality of a person's investment in a professionally helping role cannot be measured or adequately described. It is known by its results, not in its announcement. Whatever the results, the AJC Girls' Residence derived its particular character and "mix" from the investment and performance of its particular director.

The
Research

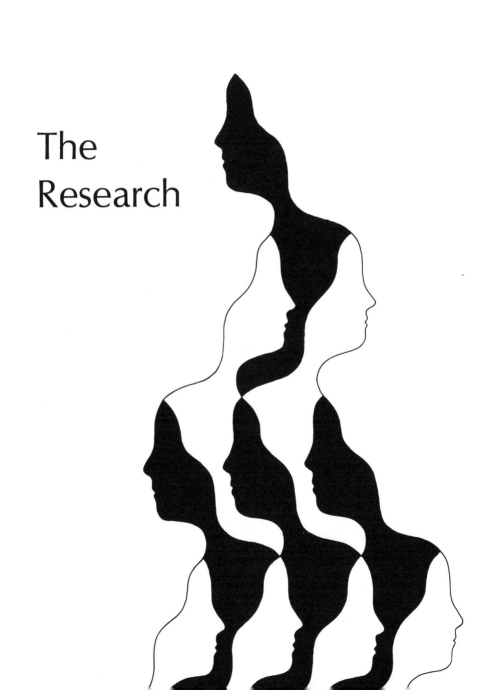

Evaluation

THE OBJECTIVES

Residential treatment programs of the type outlined in the preceding sections represent significant commitments by an agency in human effort, social risk and financial outlay. At some point in the development of a program it is reasonable enough for private donors or government agencies to ask whether this heavy commitment is worthwhile. Here, of course, we run into serious philosophical, moral, social and management questions. For the kind of girl to whom residential treatment was offered in this agency, alternative possibilities for help had failed. There were few options other than letting the girls fend for themselves, a possibility unthinkable at the present stage of our society. But the nagging question rises again and again—did the agency's efforts make any difference in the lives of the girls?

Evaluation of Outcome

The evaluation study described here anticipates the serious questions of evaluation posed by Herstein (38). It goes further by considering what procedures or which characteristics of the program or staff were more or less beneficial in achieving a given outcome. The study thus also attempts to address questions on psychotherapeutic or social welfare intervention outcome studies

59

raised by Meltzoff and Kornreich (39) and Campbell (40). An extended review of literature on the evaluation process as pertains to this particular investigation is available in Kasowski (41).

Herstein (42) called for three approaches to evaluation that he gleaned from his own review of the major issues in the field:

1) Proximate over distal outcomes
2) Specificity rather than generality
3) Professionally derived rather than community-derived criteria. (43)

Herstein emphasized proximate or recent outcome results because of his concern that so many complex factors eventually come to play in the life of an individual that to expect changes influenced by treatment to last over a period of years was ambitious and perhaps foolhardy. The present study, initiated some years before publication of Herstein's paper, proposed to ascertain whether the effectiveness of a minimum of 2 years of residential treatment could be discerned as much as 5 years after completion of the girls' stay in the residence.

Emphasis on Particular Behavioral Dimensions

The second feature of an evaluation study that Herstein called for—specificity—was in keeping with the intent of our study. It was considered especially important to relate the pattern of changes expected in girls undergoing treatment to a set of initial goals such as those developed in the earlier sections of this monograph. The sophisticated child care worker and professional can no longer rely on global concepts of adjustment such as "cure" or "total adjustment." Human personality is a complex interaction between long-standing predispositions, cognitive styles and affective patterns, and a variety of differentially demanding social settings. To talk of changing the "total personality" is vainglorious and self-deceptive. It permits one to offer hope where society prevents realization of such hope, and it also deludes both therapist and patient by focusing on such vague aspects of human change as to make evaluation subject more to wish than to reality.

In contrast to some previous studies, therefore, this study sought to evaluate the influence of the institution upon the girls along five dimensions of possible change. One might expect, in keeping with the intentions of the program, that certain types of change would be more prominent than others. In addition, it was thought that making decisions about change would be easier for objective professionals who had no personal knowledge of the intentions of the study. It was important that evaluators be "blind" as to the specific conditions of the girls whose current life situations they were expected to rate in relation to their behavior and prospects at the outset of treatment.

Judgments by Uninvolved Professionals

This question of evaluation by professionals points to the third facet of this outcome study in keeping with Herstein's call. By relying on dimensions already established in previous evaluation studies, and obviously also relevant to the objectives of the residential program, as outlined earlier, this study focused on the professional judgment of outcome, rather than seeking to meet a community-derived criterion. In addition, judgments of outcome were based on detailed reports obtained from the girls themselves during an intensive interview. These interview protocols were rated by professionals who all had experience with residential treatment centers and with long-term evaluation. None knew the girls or was familiar with the agency or the program in question. They were called on to evaluate independently the admission protocols of the 24 girls and subsequently the reports based on the followup interviews without any identifying data. They rated only with carefully worked out definitions of the five major dimensions as their guides.

The study thus permits evaluation of the extent to which professionals, in this case social workers and psychologists, can agree about material of this kind. It also permits an eventual pooling of these ratings to provide a consensual judgment about change that is free of the inevitable biases that haunt the judgments of the workers most closely invested in a given helping enterprise. We would not minimize the serious concern with objectivity that may characterize most responsible professionals in the areas of psychotherapy and social intervention; yet there is ample research evidence that the investment of effort in itself demands some wished-for reinforcement by at least modest success. The present study sought to control such possibilities by its design. By keeping the ratings of initial presenting problems and subsequent outcomes far apart, by not revealing to the raters the identity of specific girls, and by mixing other data of this kind, ratings designed to maintain self-consistency and demonstrations of improvement to ingratiate the auspices of the study could be minimized. Such tendencies would only increase the "error variance" in the statistical design.

Another major objective was to examine the process of treatment in more detail than had been possible in earlier studies of residential treatment. This called for an analysis of the components of the group home and of its staff that seemed especially influential to the participants in the program. Using the girls' own spontaneous or elicited comments, we obtained information about which individuals and which features of the program seemed especially significant (positively and negatively) to the girls. This method not only was an important part of an evaluation, but could point the way toward critical modification of the residential program itself. Such a procedure might well be built into any intervention program from the outset.

Predicted Outcome Method

A subsidiary but methodologically significant feature of the study was the effort to provide an alternative to the traditional control group that has been considered essential for evaluation of intervention procedures. The necessity for control groups is obvious, of course, in the development of intervention in the treatment of medical problems. Will a patient who has a common cold get better in 3 or 4 days without the ministrations of a physician, let alone without a prescription for medication? The evidence on that count is fairly plain and the data are easy to obtain. But to the question of whether severely troubled girls who come to a social agency modify their behavior over the years as a function of agency intervention, or simply because they have matured, no easy answer is available. Ideally, if each girl had an identical twin sister who presented the same complaints, one might deny treatment to one set of siblings and cast them adrift to determine 7 years later how they fared by comparison with their sisters. But society is not prepared to adopt such a "pure science" position, and controlled studies involving untreated patients are rarely available in the psychological or social welfare fields.

An alternative to the use of untreated controls was attempted in the present study. A group of professionals who had experience with the type of girl and the type of setting involved made predictions about the outcomes with and without social agency intervention. The professionals based their predictions in part on their experience with a variety of girls within the same age group and within the area of emotional problems manifested by these girls. In addition, most of the professionals had experience in research on psychotherapeutic outcomes or long-range follow-ups. Thus, a major objective of this research was to ascertain whether one might at least approximate the possibility of a controlled study by the method of predicted outcomes. The reader will have to judge whether the method is promising since, after all, no actual criterion is available for comparison with the predictions of our experts.

THE PROCEDURE

Outcome Evaluation

At the time the study was initiated 28 girls had completed the program and moved on. It was possible to contact all but one. Twenty-five expressed willingness to cooperate, but only 24 were involved in the study, since one was living in California and could not be interviewed. She did fill out a questionnaire. Only two girls indicated an unwillingness to participate in the study. An examination of adjustment ratings upon admission assigned the girls who did not participate does not indicate any clear pattern. Three of the nonparticipants were below average in admission ratings on the various dimensions. They had left the institution quickly because of severe behavior problems. One girl had been rated at intake as somewhat above average.

The average age upon entry into the group home for the 24 girls was 15, with a range from 12 to 16. Prior to placement at AJC, 19 of the girls had experienced some form of placement; 10 had been in foster homes, four in boarding schools, three in residential treatment and two in mental hospitals. One girl had had eight prior placements. Most girls stayed in the residence more than 2 years, some staying as long as 4. The average age at discharge was 17½. At the time of followup the average age for the girls was 22½. The average period following discharge from the group home at the time of followup interview was 5 years, with a range from 3 through 11.

All of the girls from the original sample of 28 were born into intact families. By the time of admission, however, only six came from intact homes. By that time half of the families were involved in separation or divorce and the remaining girls had at least one deceased parent. Twenty-two girls came from families with Jewish parents, and the other two had Jewish fathers. The predominant admission diagnosis was "personality disorder," with 61% showing some pattern of this kind; another 11% were described as "depressive-neurotic" and 21% were termed "schizophrenic," with the remainder diagnosed as having "adolescent adjustment reaction." The intellectual level of the girls was slightly above average. None was evaluated as retarded; one was rated as having borderline intelligence, 14 (50%) scored in the average range (IQs of 90-109); eight (28.6%) were classified as bright-normal (110-119) and five (17.9%) as superior (120-129).

The followup procedure took this form:

After an initial letter was sent out to locate the girls, letters, postcards and telephone calls were used to set up a rendez-vous. Each girl was individually interviewed in a place she chose. The interviewer was not an employee of the agency, but was a clinical psychologist with interview experience. The interview was tape-recorded and lasted more than 2 hours. The vast majority of interviews took place in the girls' homes. The interviewer made it clear from the start that she was not connected with the agency and that all statements by the girl would be kept confidential and at no time revealed to the staff of the agency; all of the protocols have in fact been anonymously labeled and scored, and have never been available to agency personnel. There is, of course, no guarantee that the girls accepted completely these statements of confidentiality. Still, the candor of their responses to the interviewer's questions and their willingness to provide material that included negative or critical details of their experiences as residents suggest that the interview material is relatively free from any self-perceived coercion from the agency.

The Interview Protocol

The followup interview included a detailed, structured section for obtaining information about the girls' current marital status, family relationships, educational level, further psychotherapy if any, and other relatively clear-cut background data. After this the interview moved somewhat more freely, but was designed to cover the five major areas that were eventually to be scored as the dimensions for evaluation of the protocols. The girls were encouraged to describe their current life situation in detail. They were permitted to elaborate in any direction they chose, but the interviewer made sure to come back to areas relevant to the dimensions of job or school performance, current living situation, and peer relationships. A detailed description of the physical setting in which the girls lived was included by the interviewer.

The interview then reviewed specific experiences of the girls during their stay in the AJC residence. Here, again, the anecdotal reports of the girls were supplemented by asking them to present their most salient memories of their experiences in the group home. These spontaneous memories were later examined in terms of their affective patterning and also in terms of content relevant to particular figures in the program. Following the spontaneous recollections, elicited memories were obtained from each girl with relation to various components of her experience. These components included memories about the total program, the peer group, the director of the residence, the caseworker, the psychiatrist and the child care staff. Memories were also obtained in relation to other features such as the community setting of the Girls' Residence.

Evaluation of the Intake Protocols

For each girl there was available a psychological testing report, usually including intelligence and projective test information as summarized by a psychologist, a psychiatric evaluation and an intake caseworker's summary. These materials, edited to avoid identification of subjects or of the agency, were made available to the judges for ratings on five dimensions. The judges were required to employ behavioral criteria in making their evaluations, and to avoid an attempt at "deep" interpretation, a procedure that might lead to considerable confusion, since the judges were not necessarily all of the same theoretical persuasion. The judges' task involved a careful reading of the intake data and a rating of each of the girls on the following variables:

1) Job or School Adequacy
2) Adjustment to General Daily Living
3) Peer Relationships—Female
4) Peer Relationships—Male
5) Self-Attitude.

These dimensions represent the areas of experience most closely related to the objectives of the group home program. The importance of such baseline admissions evaluations has been stressed by Shyne (44), Gil (45) and Fanshel (46).

Each dimension was rated on a scale from 1 to 11. Careful definitions of various points on the scale were presented to the judges and examples of protocols that might be rated in various dimensions were provided to them as part of a private training procedure. A detailed account of the dimensions and their derivation from earlier research is presented in Kasowski (47). Judges had an opportunity to practice on protocols that were not employed in the study, as a means of improving the judges' understanding of the definitions and dimensions employed.

In effect, the girls were rated for Job or School Adequacy, Peer

Relationships, Daily Living Adjustment, and Self-Attitude on the basis of all of the data available at intake. They were then evaluated on these five dimensions on the basis of their interview responses reflecting their status at least 5 years after intake. In the study, then, the basic data used in the evaluation involved the five dimensions as rated independently by judges unfamiliar with the hypotheses, with the agency, or with other details of the study. The judges did not know whether there had been any intervention procedures with the girls, since judges could not identify the same girl on both pre and post conditions. (See appendix for definitions of scales and instructions to raters.)

Evaluation of the Outcome Ratings:
The Predicted Outcome Method

The data with respect to possible control were obtained by having the raters examine intake reports and evaluate the girls' status on the five dimensions on an 11-point scale. The raters made judgments as to what score a particular girl might attain 5 years later without any social or psychotherapeutic intervention. This rating was called Predicted Outcome Without Intervention. The second rating in this initial phase was a prediction of the optimal outcome for a girl presenting this pattern of complaints and life stress who had the benefit of social welfare intervention and psychotherapy. This measure was termed Predicted Outcome With Optimal Intervention. The concept of optimal intervention encouraged the judges to set realistic goals for what first-rate therapeutic programs might offer rather than absolute idealistic goals. The concept asked the judges to consider, from our present state of knowledge, what could conceivably be accomplished using internal agency and community resources for ameliorating emotional disturbance. For the post-treatment interview material, the raters scaled the girl's current level of adjustment along the five dimensions, on the basis of the girl's own report to the interviewer.

These rating procedures permitted comparisons between the ratings the girl was assigned at her initial presentation to the AJC when she was approximately 14 and those based on her situation along the same five dimensions as revealed in interviews 3-11 years after her termination with AJC. The differences in ratings are of interest in themselves. To what extent do the girls show increases or decreases or no change at all in the ratings assigned them by the judges on the basis of their self-presentation so many years apart? But, as indicated earlier, the argument could be raised that such changes might occur simply by maturation or change produced by the passage of time. The Predicted Outcome ratings represent an alternative comparison. The subjects can then be viewed in terms of how reasonably expert judges regard their likely outcome without social welfare intervention or therapeutic exposure. Such predictions can be compared with what the same judges think might be the best possible realistic outcome for girls as severely disturbed as these were at the start. Statistical procedures to examine the various relationships among these four sets of ratings are presented in the section on results.

Evaluation Ratings: Process Data

A second set of ratings was based on interviews with the girls that included memories of life in the institution. As noted, these memories were obtained spontaneously and then were elicited specifically in relation to components of the institutional program —the role of the director, the role of the psychiatrist, the role of the social worker, the housemother, the involvement with the community, the influence of peers, etc.

To avoid contaminating the intake and outcome ratings of the group of judges, this set of memories was separated from the material available for the outcome ratings and was rated by other judges. Two judges had the relatively simple task of ascertaining whether the spontaneous memories applied to one of the listed categories—peers, director, etc. Another pair of judges then rated each memory on its affective quality, positive to negative. In addition, memories relating to specific components of the program were rated on positive or negative affect. Separate reliability evaluations were obtained for this task, which, however, proved simpler and yielded higher agreement between independent ratings for the two raters. These ratings were carried out by graduate students and a professor in clinical psychology with experience in this area.

The Judges for Intake and Outcome Ratings

It was agreed to maintain the anonymity of the judges, but it can be indicated that all seven had considerable professional maturity. Three were social workers who had worked in agencies of this kind with similar types of girls and had been concerned with followup issues to some extent. Of the psychologists, all had also worked in similar institutions and were familiar with outcome research, and, in at least two cases, were individuals who had carried out outcome studies in other areas relating to this general problem. Each rater worked independently with carefully screened protocols, and the raters at no time met with each other or knew each other's names. They were asked for qualitative comments about each girl, and for general comments or criticisms about the material they were rating. Most found the task somewhat difficult but were intrigued by the material, since each girl in the study was unique and the detailed histories obtained both at intake and from the interviews were psychologically interesting.

THE RESULTS

Reliability of Ratings

Reliability data for current adjustment for the raters were evaluated by the more conventional Pearson r statistic and the Cicchetti C (1972). The latter method is relatively new and has the advantage of taking into account the extent of agreement between individual pairs of rankings as well as the overall ordering of rankings. With both approaches, reliability for the ratings carried out by the seven judges, based on comparisons of pairs of raters and on the total sample of the study, is highly significant. Summary statistics for interrater reliability correlations are rarely

TABLE I
MEANS ON RATING SCALES FOR RESIDENCE GIRLS (N = 24)

	Intake	Predicted Outcome Without Intervention	Predicted Outcome With Optimal Intervention	Actual Outcome
1. Job or School Adequacy	5.408	4.948	6.992	5.719
2. Adjustment to General Daily Living	4.742	4.417	6.600	5.869
3. Peer Relationships—Female	5.008	4.865	6.742	5.929
4. Peer Relationships—Male	4.200	3.792	6.108	4.885
5. Self-Attitude	4.667	4.250	6.467	5.229
Total Adjustment	4.805	4.454	6.582	5.526

lower than .80. Scale 1, Job or School Adequacy, shows the highest overall ratings for the Current, Prediction/With, Prediction/ Without Intervention and followup scores. Rating reliabilities therefore are quite satisfactory.

The ratings for group home adjustment and the affective memory-tone scales, based on the subjects' recollections and ratings by the two graduate student judges involved, yielded extremely high levels of reliability ($p < .001$) for each scale. For a sample of ratings carried out on 52 memories produced by subjects evaluated independently by two judges, the reliabilities yielded a C statistic and a Pearson r both significant at $p < .001$.

Evaluation of Outcome

We confront now the heart of the research. As against their initial evaluations on the five dimensions, how did the girls end up on the basis of the estimates made by the judges? The first relevant item is the initial rating of most of the girls on the 11-point scale on each of the dimensions. Figure 1 and Table I show the summary of the average ratings of the girls on the five psychosocial scales employed. The average rating is low, approximately 4.8 on the 11-point scale. The Actual Outcome score shows that, a decade later, the average rating is by no means high, being close to 5.5.

In terms of shifts in level of the individual girls, one can look at the average of the five separate scales for a given girl to provide a picture of her "total" adjustment. At intake five girls (21%) showed "slight overall adjustment" (a score of 3), 11 girls (46%) "some adjustment" (a score of 5) and eight (33%) were rated at "average overall adjustment." At followup the shift is obvious—five girls (21%) were still at "slight adjustment," only six (25%) at "some adjustment," while 11 (46%) were rated at "average adjustment" and two (8%) at "very good adjustment." An analysis of variance of the scores of the girls for "total adjustment" yields a significance level of $p = .01$, indicating that the upward shift in ratings from intake to outcome is statistically reliable and not attributable to chance variation.

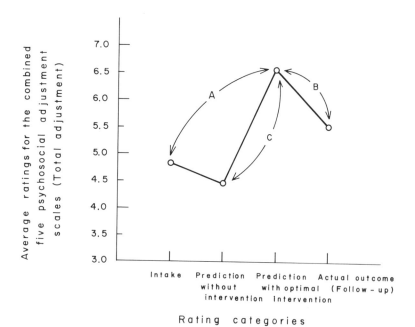

Figure 1. Scores of the girls (N = 24) averaged across the five psychosocial adjustment scales for four rating categories (Total adjustment).

(Note: For statistical comparisons: A = Prediction with Optimal Intervention—Intake; B = Prediction with Optimal Intervention—Actual Outcome on followup; C = Prediction with Optimal Intervention—Prediction without Intervention. C > B; A > B.)

One question that arises is whether there were any relationships among the five separate dimensions. If all of them were highly correlated, one might question the value of using separate dimensions. The intercorrelations for the five dimensions rated (Job or School Adequacy; Adjustment to General Daily Living; Peer Relationships—Female; Peer Relationships—Male; and Self-Attitude) were statistically reliable but moderate in degree for almost all combinations of conditions. Of the five dimensions, only Self-Attitude showed a pattern of sufficiently high correlation with all other variables to suggest that it might reflect an overall adjustment factor.

An analysis of variance was undertaken to determine whether the psychosocial adjustment scores varied significantly with the assessment periods (i.e., from intake prediction to followup) by scales (i.e., along the five psychosocial adjustment scales), and whether there was an interaction between scales and assessment periods. The F ratios for both assessment periods and scales were significant beyond the .01 level. Interaction effects were not significant, indicating that the *scale × assessment period* combinations contributed no unique effects. This test suggests that we may now move to an examination of the specific changes along each dimension for the girls, using the t test to evaluate the comparison of the girls' score initially with their Actual Outcome score. It is necessary to take into account that each girl's initial score limits the possible changes she could make. The required statistic is the t test for differences within subjects.

There were highly significant increases from the time of intake to followup in three of the five dimensions and a nearly significant increase in a fourth dimension. The significant increases were in Adjustment to General Daily Living Situation ($t = 3.19$, $p < .005$); in Relationships With Peers—Female ($t = 3.35$, $p < .003$); and Self-Attitude ($t = 2.58$, $p < .014$). Relationships With Peers—Male barely missed significance ($t = 1.81$, $p < .083$) and there was no significant improvement in Job or School Adequacy ($t = 308$, $p < .5$). The consistency of the changes is impressive and clearly not attributable to chance effects.

One might have expected some differences between the separate dimensions in which improvements took place. A comparison of the scores on followup with those from intake suggests that

the most significant changes took place in the areas of Adjustment to General Daily Living, Relationship With Peers—Female, and Self-Attitude. This analysis remains subject to the
question of whether such improvements might not have occurred
without any intervention efforts, simply as a function of life
changes and social maturity. Really sizable gains in Job or School
Adequacy were probably limited by the fact that at intake the
girls showed their highest scores in this area already. We need,
therefore, to consider the possible alternative outcomes that the
judges predicted for these girls on the basis of their intake interview data.

Predicted Outcomes With and Without Intervention

What did the judges really expect for these girls without any
intervention? Figures 1 and 2 and Table I indicate that the consensus raters anticipated a moderate reduction in adjustment
levels over time on the various dimensions. Examination of the
separate dimensions indicates that the predictions were for significant reductions in Job or School Adequacy ($t = 1.94$, $p = .05$)
and highly significant reductions in adequacy for the other four
dimensions—Adjustment to General Daily Living ($t = 3.83$,
$p < .001$); Peer Relationships—Female ($t = 3.11$; $p = .005$); and
Self-Attitude ($t = 3.50$, $p < .002$). The judges predicted a worsen-
ing in the social adjustment and self-esteem of these girls as they
confronted the more complex problems of early womanhood.
Apparently they assumed the maturation would limit the decline
of the girls' abilities in work situations.

Table I and Figure 2 also indicate that the scores for Predicted
Outcome With Optimal Intervention assigned by the judges were
obviously highest. Still, the overall rating system was based on
an 11-point scale, and the best hope for these girls was an average score of 6.5. One cannot accuse the judges of being unrealistic. All of the differences between intake adjustment scores
on the five dimensions and the Predicted Outcome With Optimal
Intervention scores are highly statistically significant. As is obvious from the figures, the patterns of Predicted Outcome Without
Intervention and Predicted Outcome With Optimal Intervention

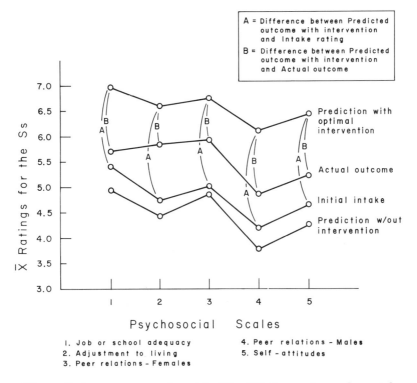

Figure 2. Average scores for girls (N = 24) for each psychosocial scale and rating category.

(Note: For statistical analyses. A = Predicted Outcome With Optimal Intervention—Intake ratings, B = Predicted Outcome With Optimal Intervention—Actual Outcome on followup. Thus A should always be greater than B if results are beneficial.)

are widely separated and the data are reliably different by statistical tests, with all p-values well below .001. This result indicates that the judges' consensus of ratings yielded a clear separation between the prospects they held out for these girls with and without social welfare intervention.

Outcomes Compared With Predictions

We next examine whether the scores assigned the girls at followup are significantly greater than the scores predicted for them without any therapeutic intervention. This is the equivalent of looking at what happened to an untreated control group. Here the results indicate a marginally significant change for the Job or School Adequacy dimension ($p < .065$), but highly significant differences for the other four dimensions, with p-values all less than .005.

How close were the Predicted Outcome With Optimal Intervention scores to the Actual Outcome ratings for the girls? If the treatment were ideally effective, one ought to find no differences between the ratings on the dimensions and these predictions. This, however, is not the case for every dimension. The differences between the Predicted Outcome With Optimal Intervention and the Actual Outcome scores are strongly significant. In other words, the judges expected the girls to do better under optimal intervention procedures than they actually did more than 5 years after their first contact with the agency. The girls' improvement with the help of the AJC program was not so great as was hoped for by reasonably tough-minded experts. Keep in mind that optimal expectation scores were still well below the top levels on the rating scales.

Perhaps a more critical and subtle test of the effects of the treatment program emerges if we next examine whether the difference between the two predictions (with and without intervention) is reliably greater than the difference between the Predicted Outcome With Optimal Intervention scores and the Actual Outcome scores. If we grant that the judges may have been overly optimistic, one might expect the gap between their most hopeful and least hopeful prediction for change to be significantly greater than the gap between their most optimistic expectation and the Actual Outcome result. Statistical analysis reveals that the actual result for these girls was significantly closer to the ideal predicted result on all of the five dimensions. Results for each of the five dimensions are significant, with p-values all less than .001. In effect, although the girls did not do so well as one might have hoped, they ended up significantly closer to the ideal than the difference between the best and worst predicted outcomes. (See Figure 1, Comparison C-B).

Probably the most critical test of the findings comes from examining the differences between the Intake ratings of behavior of the subject and the Predicted Outcome With Optimal Intervention, to see if that gap is greater than the difference that emerges between the followup Actual Outcome and the Predicted Outcome With Optimal Intervention. Again, this comparison, which is diagrammed in Figures 1 and 2 (Comparisons A-B), yields highly significant results for each of the five dimensions. In all cases differences are highly significant, with p = value less than .001 for each dimension. That is, the separation in scores between how the girls ended up and the ideal scores predicted for them was much smaller than the gap between where they started from and where the judges predicted they might end up under best treatment.

In effect, these analyses suggest that, although the girls who completed the program did not do so well as the judges hoped they might do with a therapeutic program, they came reasonably close to that ideal. The difference between their performance and the ideal predicted outcome is still not so great as the difference between either the predicted outcome for the girls without any treatment and the ideal situation, or the difference between their initial status on admission and the predicted ideal therapeutic outcome. It seems reasonable to interpret these findings as supportive of a substantial influence for the better on these girls' lives by the group home treatment program. This is all the more noteworthy if we keep in mind that so many complex life circumstances are likely to have intervened to produce negative as well as positive possibilities for the girls in the years between completion of the program and evaluation. This analysis also suggests that the predicted outcome technique used in this study adds substantially to our understanding of the change in the dimensions of the personal adjustment for the girls, compared with what we find simply from an examination of intake and followup scores without any sense of what might be expected under control conditions.

In studies such as these there is always a possibility that what might be called "ceiling" effects could play a role in limiting how much improvement it is possible to show. Since it is obvious that even under ideal circumstances the judges did not anticipate much more than a slightly above-average adjustment for all of the girls, one could raise the question as to whether the improvement of those girls who showed an initially relatively high level of adjustment would be limited in possible change in relation to the ideal outcome. We can examine this possibility by dividing the total sample into two groups of girls, those with above-average initial adjustment scores (in this case totaling all scores for the five dimensions) and those with below-average initial adjustment scores. Graphing these relationships between Intake, Predicted Outcome Without Intervention, Predicted Outcome With Optimal Intervention and Actual Outcome evaluation scores separately (Figure 3), shows that the changes for the low adjustment girls were much more dramatic than those for the high adjustment girls. The difference between the ideal predicted outcome and actual outcome is significantly lower for the low initial adjustment girls than it is for the girls with initially high adjustment scores. An analysis of variance evaluation of the adjustment levels by rating periods yields an F-ratio of 1.80 for 12 d.f. with a p-value of .05. (See Figure 3, Comparison Ah-Bh and AL-BL).

At least for this sample, a case could be made that the greatest benefit of the group home came for the more disturbed group of girls initially admitted. The girls, and particularly the initially poorly adjusted ones, made especially strong progress in their day-to-day adjustment to the details of self-organization, running of their personal lives and households. This result substantiates a major thrust of the general program of the AJC Girls' Residence. It indicates that the emphasis placed on details of personal grooming, physical attention to health and other aspects of daily life care, on which particular stress was put in the plan

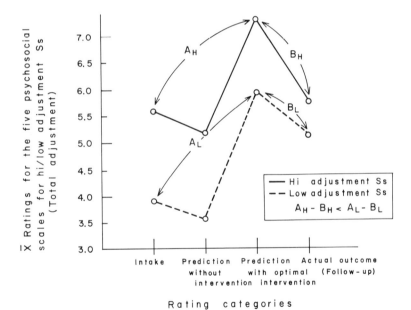

Figure 3. Total adjustment scores on the various rating categories for girls divided at median into high and low adjustment at the time of initial Intake.

(A_H = Predicted outcome with optimal intervention for high intake adjustment girls—Initial Intake score. . . . . . Statistical analysis involves $A_H - B_H < A_L - B_L$.)

for the residents, was especially successful in comparison with what might have been predicted without intervention or, relative to other factors of adjustment, what was predicted with ideal intervention. Although the most substantial improvement for the girls came in the area of relationship to female peers, this was more or less expected for these girls. Again, the improvement in relationships with male peers and in self-attitude is somewhat greater in relation to the five adjustment measures than might have been anticipated.

Some effects of initial entry factors or discharge pattern upon outcome may be briefly cited. What of the effect on outcome of the girls' intelligence levels at admission, for example? If the sample is divided into girls scoring above average to superior in IQ and those scoring at average IQ levels or slightly below, the data show that the brighter girls were rated as better off in Total Adjustment at Intake. In the followup, gains for above-average and average IQ girls were fairly similar, however. The brighter girls were significantly more likely to report that the group home program was beneficial, however, ($p < .05$).

To what extent did the girls' ability to get along with the day-to-day requirements of the group home play a role in the eventual outcome? Three components of adjustment to the group home were identified, Relations With Adults, Relations With Peers, and Task Performance. As might be expected, those girls rated higher in overall adjustment at Intake were more successful in handling residential living requirements. Nevertheless, the adjustment to the institution itself was not predictive of subsequent adjustment. There was no differential in improvement simply on the basis of how well the girls got along in the institution. In other words, despite troublesome times in the setting, many of the initially most poorly adjusted girls were able to make substantial gains, especially in relation to what experts predicted for them.

Although intactness of own home does not relate to outcome, the degree of planning for discharge from the group home does have a measurable impact on later adjustment. The six girls in the evaluation sample who left precipitously (without careful agency planning) were compared with 18 who left with careful planning. The followup Total Adjustment scores were significantly higher ($p < .05$) for the planned discharge group.

Statistical and Qualitative Outcome Findings

It may be useful to look at some characteristics of the more general living situation of these girls as determined in the followup. Twelve (42.9%) of the group home's residents returned to live with members of their immediate families after their somewhat more than 2 years in the group home. By the followup interview practically all of the girls in the study were living either with husbands or children or with female roommates. Only six were living alone and three lived with parents. About 60% of the girls were still single at followup. Eleven girls had married and eight had borne children. Of those that married, five had been divorced, two separated and one divorced and remarried. The frequency of breakup of marriages or nonmarital living arrangements is probably not remarkable for girls coming from so disturbed a social background, or, indeed, for this youthful generation. At followup only one girl was married to and rearing her children with the natural father and one other was rearing a child with the common-law natural father. Four girls were rearing their children without males in the home and two others had given their children up for foster care or adoption. This general result is not greatly encouraging, but again it has to be viewed to some extent within the context of what has happened to the entire generation of troubled adolescents from the mid-1960s, a period of traumatic social change.

The results in education are much more positive, and represent to some extent a major area in which the group home had potential for influence. More than half of the girls had substantial college experience and another 12% had completed high school. Of the eight girls who dropped out of high school, five did so while at the group home and were referred to facilities such as the Jewish Employment Vocational Service for job planning and training. Two received training in beauty culture and computer work and two others received general skills training. The fifth girl left the group home before training began. Only three girls who dropped out after completing the group home program received no further vocational training.

At the time of followup, only about 20% of the girls were employed in responsible positions, but a majority were either full-time students or engaged in full-time child care, and only three girls were unemployed. Although the girls' average income was generally low (below $3500 a year) this was in part because many were full-time students. Only four girls of the 24 were on public assistance. One-third of the girls had average incomes well above $5000 a year. Again, this result compares adequately with girls of this age coming from lower middle class or upper lower class socioeconomic levels.

None of the girls was hospitalized for emotional disturbance or was arrested after discharge from the group home. Seven girls had brief psychotherapy—less than a year—in the interim period, but most had no further treatment and were not contemplating it. Only one girl had any significant involvement with drugs—a "speed" habit that she overcame a year after her discharge from the residence. A few girls smoked marijuana moderately on social occasions. The general level of drug use and certainly of drug abuse seemed substantially below that indicated for lower socio-economic group girls of that generation.

In summary, this review of outcome suggests that these girls, who began with extremely limited emotional and personal or social resources, were making their way in the world with some effectiveness. Few were dependent on welfare or mental health services. In comparison with what had been predicted for them, in the lack of any help, on the basis of their intake evaluations by the judges, these girls were coping in society in a substantially more effective manner. Intake reviews by the judges had led to predictions that without intervention a sizable number would find their way to state hospitals; this clearly proved not to be the case. In the main, the girls developed independent lives, a major positive result. That they found "happiness" and entered the idealized mainstream of bourgeois family life cannot be maintained. But were such prospects even thinkable for these girls at the outset of their contacts with the agency? By the age of 23 many girls from lower middle class or upper lower class urban backgrounds with badly split families have not done well in entering the middle class mainstream. Viewed against the major objectives of the AJC program, e.g., the development of the capacity for independent social adjustment, for adequate personal care and for avoiding further social disorganization and hospitalization, these girls have achieved reasonable independence. They are working out lives entirely free of dependence on the courts and mental health system and relatively free of the welfare system.

Adjustment to the Residence Program

Spontaneous Recollection Data

The girls were asked during the followup interview to provide three spontaneous memories about their stay in the group home. Twenty girls complied and produced 60 spontaneous memories. The memories were evaluated on a 7-point scale measuring affective tone. Almost three-quarters of the memories concerned relationships with the other girls. The only other substantial number of memories related to the director (17) and to the child care staff (13). Using the salience of memories as an indicator of important influences in the group home experience, relationships among the girls emerge as the most significant factor. By this measure, the psychiatrist and caseworker appear as much less significant figures.

Ratings of the emotional characteristics of these recollections indicate that 65% were negatively toned and 30% positive, the rest showing mixed affects. Regarding the *elicited* memories, four of the seven components received a majority of positive recollections. These were the physical characteristics of the house, the neighboring community, the peer group in the home and the caseworker. A majority of the girls reported negative memories about housemothers, psychiatrists and the director. It is noteworthy that the affective tone of 17 of the 20 *elicited* memories concerning the director were negative.

Evaluation of Overall Program and Its Components

Fifty-nine percent of the girls reported that the program had been of moderate to significant benefit for them. With respect to specific components, 73% of the respondents indicated that the contact with the director had been of moderate to significant help, 71% specified that the peer group contact had been of moderate to significant help, 48% reported benefit from contact with the caseworker, and 31% and 18%, respectively, reported at least moderate benefit from contact with the psychiatrist or child care workers. If one takes the highest level of benefit, "significant benefit" ("could not have gotten along without help received") as a criterion, the peer group emerges as the most valued component. Statistical analysis indicates that the girls evaluated contacts with the child care staff as significantly less beneficial than contacts with the peer group, the director and the overall residence program. The peer group was also perceived as having had significantly greater impact than the psychiatric service. In general there was a correlation between the elicited memories and the girls' appraisal of the situation, with one exception. In the case of the director, although elicited memories almost always involved a negative emotional tone, the girls evaluated the director in her role performance as the most helpful and influential individual in the entire program.

Content of Elicited Memories

The Director

An informal investigation of the substantive content of elicited memories revealed that three-quarters of the recollections concerning the director described conflict with authority. The memories included the criticism and the discipline the director used to aid the girls to adapt socially, e.g., to go to school, to do homework, to keep clean physically, to avoid undesirable boys, to stop cursing and abusing the child care staff, etc. Though the director was portrayed as overly concerned with discipline and misdeeds, the girls nevertheless expressed a considerable liking, respect and admiration for the director and for the many responsibilities she carried. Apparently the girls adopted a relatively realistic view of the director's role and recognized that she was called in when other disciplinary resources failed during acts of rebellion. Within this framework, her role seemed to them in the long run a helpful one. The director emerged as the one person whom the girls described at followup as someone they could eventually return to or call upon for help if it was needed years after.

The Psychiatric Staff

In about half of the memories girls were depicted as either in conflict with the psychiatrist concerning an interpretation, or in direct confrontation, or unable to communicate with the psychiatrist. Four of the 15 girls who contributed memories of psychiatric contacts were in treatment with therapists in outside organizations. These girls' memories and direct evaluations of treatment were more positive than those of girls treated by the agency psychiatrist. Similarly, more girls treated outside the agency felt that their psychiatric contacts were at least moderately beneficial.

Six of the 15 recollections concerning the psychiatrists were positive. Positive features included support during periods of emotional stress and an elucidating interpretation. Of the nine negative recollections, almost all depicted girls as disagreeing with the therapist's viewpoint (regarding a confrontation, interpretation, perceived manipulation, etc.), or being unable to communicate with her. Despite their generally negative recollections of the psychiatrist and caseworker, about half the girls said they had received some help with emotional difficulties in the form of increased awareness of self or others in a specific problem area. Ten girls specifically minimized the value of psychotherapy as part of the overall program.

The Casework Staff

The girls took a generally positive view of the caseworker and particularly recalled the caseworker's interest in their concerns, her companionship and her tolerance for their tendencies toward

overt aggression. They expressed some negative reactions to conflicts over planning and an occasional sense that confidentiality
had not been protected. The major reaction by the girls indicated that they viewed the caseworker as less powerful and
hence less threatening than either the director or the psychiatric
staff. In general, the girls did not place great importance on the
role of the caseworker in the overall benefit obtained from the
group home program. To some extent they seemed to feel that
the caseworker's influence was undercut because of the key role
the director played at times of disciplinary crisis.

The Child Care Staff

Only a few memories concerning the child care workers were
positive in tone, and these generally involved one-to-one interactions, talking over problems during periods of crisis or visits to
the child care workers' living quarters. Most of the negative recollections concerned conflicts over food, acts of overt aggression
toward a child care worker, disappointment over the child care
workers' failure to understand the girls' feelings. Particularly lacking was a sense that the girls viewed the child care staff as providing a nurturing environment and as gratifying the more basic
or dependent needs. The memories convey an impression that
the child care staff did not supply the kind of day-to-day psychological nurturing that the girls hoped for.

The Peer Group

The majority of memories concerning the other girls involved
pleasant interactions with residence mates. The girls recalled
specific recreational activities, close friends, or situations in which
peers give them special attention. The negative memories particularly involved their anxiety when witnessing another girl's
difficulties, occasional aggressive interactions, or group disobedi-
ence. Even where difficult peer relationships were acknowledged (and over half of the girls admitted at least one troublesome peer relationship), they tended to be glossed over. The
staff was much more likely to be the scapegoat. This finding
seems important, bearing in mind that the girls apparently found

even among their troubled peers some affiliation group or some focus of reference and identification.

Overall Evaluation of the Effect of the Residence

Approximately half of the girls spontaneously stated that they had received some help with emotional difficulties while at the group home. This took the form of increased awareness of and sensitivity to others. The girls also mentioned help in specific problem areas such as interpersonal relationships, information about sex and satisfying peer relationships, exposure to cultural experiences, and good physical care. With regard to negative reactions, the majority of the girls criticized what they felt was the regimented structure, the overorganized approach of the group home. They felt there had been too much emphasis on rules and regulations. Ten of the girls said the staff showed too little warmth, understanding and concern. Some references were also made by a few to the emphasis on living up to social norms, to dissatisfaction with psychotherapy and to a lack of cohesion.

Summary of Process Findings

What emerges from the process review is a conclusion that the overall influence of the residence had been moderately positive, despite much chafing about the regulations and regimentation. It is important to note that the girls referred again and again to the key role of the director and to interaction with their peers as crucial positive considerations. Positive attitudes about the community and the physical characteristics of the group home were also stressed. It is clear that the major factor that emerged qualitatively as well as quantitatively from the girls' recollections was that for many of the girls *this was their first experience living in an organized, physically attractive home within a decent community.* It is remarkable—if one compares these girls' comments with those of "normal" youngsters about camp life or college dormitory life—that there were no angry references to the quality of the food.

This experience made a lasting impression. The girls came from disorganized families and most showed severe emotional impulsivity and disorganized day-to-day patterns of living. Yet they indicated in retrospect that, however unpleasant the rules were for them, in the long run they benefited from learning how to adjust to reasonable social demands. They also found support from a peer group, something they lacked prior to admission to the residence. With so few things "going for them" the major possibilities offered by a residential setting of this kind lay in giving the girls the option of a more orderly way of life, an opportunity to learn control, an opportunity to be a part of a peer group that could clearly be identified as friendly, and at least one significant figure who represented, however strictly, a clarity of direction and concern. This figure was the director, and it may be that the emphasis in programs of this kind is best built around some such individual, a stable parent surrogate, relaxed yet firm, who offers the consistency and continuity these girls never experienced in their own families.

Conclusions

The program of the AJC Girls' Residence was constructed around a number of carefully rationalized objectives and therapeutic principles. What conclusions can be drawn from the experience of implementing these principles and evaluating their impact on the girls treated in the program?

The findings reveal a correspondence between the stated objectives of the group home program and the results achieved in the five variables selected for study.

The gains in Adjustment to General Daily Living reflect the major thrust of the program to develop personal and social competence. The girls are not only living lives free of pathology—no delinquency, no mental hospitalizations, no drugs, minor involvement for psychotherapy—but are managing their daily activities and households effectively. The program's objectives and methods emerge as particularly suited for the girls who were rated lowest on admission. Surprisingly, the girls came to feel a lot better about themselves (Self-Attitude), a conclusion based on what they said in the followup interviews and confirmed by the judgments of the case raters. Most research in psychotherapy and other treatment has found that poor self-concept is highly resistant to change. Perhaps improvement in self-image is related more to the acquisition of personal and social skills than to psychological reorientation per se.

The girls made significant gains in Peer Relationships, Female. Although gains in Peer Relationships, Male, were not so dramatic, they did approach levels considered in the original baseline ratings as attainable only with good professional help.

The absence of statistically significant improvement in School or Job Adequacy, as noted in the study, is puzzling. At the time of followup the majority of girls were either full-time students or engaged in the full-time care of children. More than half of the girls had completed, were attending or had been in college, and another 12% had completed high school. Five of eight girls who had been unable to finish high school nevertheless successfully completed vocational training programs arranged by the agency. The three girls who completed neither high school nor vocational training all left the group home program precipitously, without the benefit of agency planning. At the time of followup only three girls were unemployed. Clearly, this program either preserved the potential in School or Job Adequacy that the girls had when they entered the group home, or the program made some other contribution that was not detected in the study. Possibly "blind" judges, accustomed to even lower levels of school adjustment in the population of children found in their personal clinical experience, overrated the initial baseline school adjustments. They may have underrated the School or Job Adequacy outcome in those girls of good intelligence who came from family backgrounds that valued education despite serious trouble between parents and children.

THE PROGRAM COMPONENTS

The effort to affect the performance of the girls in the areas represented by the variables proceeded through a number of components in the treatment program. The components of the director and the peer group emerged as by far the two most important and helpful factors in the experience of the girls. This, plus the girls' recognition that the residence itself was a stable, orderly, attractive home that met all of their needs unstintingly and with dignity, suggests that the program succeeded in making therapeutic the organic parts of the group home experience, as distinguished from components, such as education, that exist outside the group home.

Memory recall was another way in which the girls were asked to evaluate their experience in the program. The validity of memory recall rests on the notion of the salience of memories, e.g., that that which is recalled is the victor in the competition that takes place in one's unconscious for what is most important to the individual psychically. There are several cautions to be observed in assessing the salience of memories. The theory is somewhat speculative. One can also question to what extent the schizophrenic girls in the study were aware of what was going on (the brighter, more intact girls were significantly more likely to evaluate the program as having been beneficial). Nevertheless, one must take the responses of the girls seriously, unless one adopts the unlikely conclusion that the girls were all wrong.

The negative memories expressed by the girls with respect to the director, the psychiatrist and in part to the child care staff were rooted predominantly in conflicts growing out of challenges to the behavior of the girls and the ensuing confrontations. These conflicts were inherent in the basic approach to treatment, which upheld a value system and concepts of right and wrong behavior. As a result the child care staff was perceived differently by the sponsors of the program and by the girls. The sponsors perceived the child care workers as successful in maintaining a warm, homelike setting, generally able to sustain attitudes of affection toward the girls, yet capable of discipline, sensitive and responsive for the most part to their needs and able to accept the hostility the girls directed toward them. It is no exaggeration to say that the child care workers were literally human punching bags for the girls, with no end to the anger the workers had to absorb. It is doubtful that anyone could have supplied affection in the degree that would have pleased these emotionally deprived adolescents, or that their psychological makeup (discussed earlier in the section on Concepts of Deprivation) could have permitted them to accept such doses of affection.

But apart from the differing perceptions in this study and the speculations they engender, the issue of child care staff is of serious concern today to the whole field of group care. No one knew for sure in 1959, and no one knows for sure today, how child care workers in various settings and with various child populations should perform and how they should be trained. At the time the

AJC program was started, the work of child care staff was held in low esteem, and it is held in only slightly higher regard today, except for some professionals in the field of group care who realize that child care workers are the backbone of residential programs. Opinions differ about the suitability of the older women who were the child care workers in the AJC program during the period of this study, and even if older women are considered desirable, the breed is dying out and hard to find. There have been many proposals for strengthening performance of child care workers—to select younger, psychologically astute, better educated, helping-career-oriented persons; to institute formal training such as 2-year college associate degree courses, group specialist training, intensive inservice instruction or interactional therapy training; to pay higher salaries to attract more able persons, and to elevate the status of the work. However, the new ideas about child care staff are still largely conjectural and judgments about them are largely impressionistic. A recent national survey of group care (47) found that although there was unanimity about the need for new approaches and models, suggestions for achieving them were indefinite and vague. Not all reports of new experiences are favorable. In one community many graduates of a 2-year university course have chosen to take jobs in less demanding fields such as day care of dependent children. Since 1970, AJC has employed a number of college-enrolled or college-graduate men and women in the group homes. Many of these young persons have fine qualities, but they do not last on the job, they create serious dislocations through turnover and they are less successful in controlling adolescents. The problem of child care staff is central to the future of all forms of group care. But the solutions will not be found in faddist espousal of right-sounding alternatives.

The questions raised by the memories about the psychiatric service involve 1) whether an intramural service is better than a service provided by community clinics, and 2) whether the particular approach to psychotherapy, which aroused negative memories generated by confrontation and interpretation or perceived manipulation, is valid. The first question arises because most of the girls who felt that their contacts with therapists were beneficial had therapists not affiliated with AJC. Unfortunately,

there is no sound basis for comparison in the first question, because 1) the intramural psychiatrist took girls who were considered less rewarding candidates for psychotherapy, and 2) there
were significant differences in the approach to treatment taken
by the intramural and the outside psychiatrists. The AJC psychiatrist was more confronting and challenging, and was identified by the girls with the control aspects of the program. The outside psychiatrists were able to be more accepting of the girls.
They knew only the girl's side of the events in the residence, and
were in no position to handle distortions and projections on an
ongoing basis.

As to the second question, the intramural psychiatric service
was started in 1960 because of serious limitations in the service
offered by community clinics. At that time Taylor (48) observed,
regarding extramural psychiatric service, that many psychiatrists
in the community clinics were reluctant to treat the girls because
they were so hostile, uncooperative and unrewarding in terms of
progress, and because the girls' needs for long-term treatment
tied up clinic hours. Moreover, since no one clinic could supply
all the treatment hours needed, the AJC program had to relate
to a variety of therapists in different clinics, who had varying
orientations to psychotherapy and varying understanding of residential treatment. The psychiatrists in clinics held contradictory
opinions about the timing and style of psychotherapy, the capacity for parenting found among the marginal type of mothers and
fathers who place their children in foster care, the value parents
hold for given children, whether given children should visit with
their parents and how often, and whether given children should
return to their parents or remain in care. The interaction with so
many therapists and their differences made it impossible for AJC
to evolve a consistent orientation to the role, goals and timing of
psychotherapy. In the course of inevitable compromises or accommodations to diverse points of view, AJC tended to lose the
self-identity that gives conviction, security and continuity to
practice.

Since the group home program was found overall to have
achieved significant benefits, since it is not possible to separate
out the relative impact of the components in any objective way,
and since the "mix" of components is assumed to be responsible

for the results achieved, no change is currently contemplated in the structure of the psychiatric service.

It would have been gratifying had the girls recalled the director, the child care staff and the psychiatrist fondly, but it is more important that the girls made significant improvement. Had the girls neither made improvement nor liked the experience of receiving help, their recollections would compel a different interpretation.

The girls' relationships with males is another area that required study. The high incidence of divorce and separation found at followup is troubling, even though it may not have been far out of line, all things considered. Nevertheless, we cannot be satisfied with the heterosexual adjustment reports.

The rabbi and the house physician provided the only male relationships through the program itself. Most of the girls had boyfriends and dating was encouraged. But the environment of the group home was largely female. True, many girls growing up today in average American families have little more in the way of male relationships. A survey released in September 1975 by the United States Department of Health, Education and Welfare found that the average American father of children age 2-12 sees his offspring 12½ minutes daily. But lacks in the average American family should not excuse lacks elsewhere, so one must ask whether the all-female environment of the group home program was a detriment. Would male staff members as caseworkers, child care workers or psychiatrist have benefited the girls psychosexually? What would be the most satisfactory or effective way to bring males onto the staff? Are there ways other than through staff for the girls to have relationships with men who would present healthy male role models? Some changes have been made in recent years. A male child care worker was employed when the group home began a three-shift, 8-hour day schedule in 1974, but the trial failed. With the expansion of the volunteer program and its Big Sister component in 1966, the girls have been encouraged to visit frequently in the volunteers' homes for the experience of being some part of a normal family, including relationships with the husbands and older sons. This area will continue to receive attention.

The notion of the predicted outcome with and without intervention as a key to evaluation seems an important contribution of the study. Would it not make sense for these measures to be employed for even more individualized goals set for a girl in relation to the specific details of a life? Agencies could well set such goals and predictions of a highly specific kind as a part of their initial evaluation and treatment process. Such a procedure might sharpen the planning and treatment goals, as well as provide a basis for followup evaluation.

Epilogue

The findings that the program had a positive impact on the girls who were treated is gratifying. It is no small accomplishment to turn a troubled human life around from failure to achievement and to transform defeat about oneself into recognition of worth. To succeed in these things consistently, as the study shows, is a noteworthy achievement. But it would be a mistake to view the help as a jump of one or two or three points on a scale. These figures are the best symbols research can produce at present to capture growth in the lives of human beings. No one will ever know precisely how much the girls were influenced by this program. The important finding is that, consistently, troubled and despairing human lives on a steady downhill course were turned around. Once that happens the way is prepared for better things to follow. Unsolicited reports from or about many of the girls since the completion of the study tell of continued progress in education, work and personal relationships.

Yet while these achievements create respect for the program, they should not be taken as the justification for it. The primary objectives of the program were humanitarian, not clinical. The public and the board of directors that established and support this program created it to provide a home for children who had no other place to go. Few children, whatever their condition or prognosis psychodynamically, are turned away. Moreover, the obligation to serve the humanitarian purpose often results in a "mix" of clinical conditions among the girls enrolled at a given time that adds to the obstacles in treatment. The objective is to fulfill the humanitarian purpose in a way that benefits the girls, but the prospects for "success" are secondary considerations. It is gratifying to learn through this study that it is possible to fulfill both objectives.

After examining the components, services, roles and techniques that were considered significant in the operation of the program, and after subjecting these factors to sophisticated research measurements, we must conclude that the fate of such programs is determined ultimately by a few intangibles that cannot be objectified, demonstrated or measured. These intangibles are values—ideas about what is important and what is right. Of all the values that motivated this program, one was fundamental and dominating. Those who designed the program believed that the individual girl was important, that she was worth saving, and that this had to be done in a way that would make her a better and more successful human being. The belief in the worth of the girls was more than an abstract moral notion. It assumed that each girl had specific qualities of worth that could be identified, nourished and translated into assets for growing up better, however hopeless the task might at times appear. The gap between that assumption and the attainment often had to be bridged by patience and sheer will, as much as by acts of program. The girl might not care about herself but the people who were helping her did, and they rarely gave up. Differences in degree do create substantive differences and there are degrees of caring commitment and tenacity of purpose. The unusual commitment of the people in this program is evident in the number of years they stayed with this hard, draining work; in the amount of time they often gave to it far beyond the normal work week; in the way they worked together, abolishing traditional differences in role and subordinating their own roles when necessary for the greater good of a girl, and channeling the ultimate authority for the program into a person—the director—who established her right to this responsibility by her personal performance and by the support she gave to the work of the others. Testimony to this point of view was given recently by Maier:

> These children require central persons in their lives who
> will nurture, support and guide them as they try to

> hurdle the problems of daily living. . . . I submit that
> children develop neither by conditioned behavior nor by
> their reflection and insight into their fears and anger;
> they develop by interpersonal engagements with each
> other and with adults. Some preliminary data support
> the view that it is neither the caring message nor the
> system of reward or punishment that constitutes the
> essence of child care work; rather, it is the experience of
> the caring person's involvement in the issues facing
> children and caring adults that really counts. (49)

A group home program must have a group commitment to the task. The ensemble is more important than the virtuoso performer. It would be naive to think that caring and commitment alone can make these programs succeed—obviously, these qualities must be joined to concepts of treatment and thoughtfully planned services—but without these qualities, residential programs for deeply disturbed children will not realize their potential.

References

(1) Martin Gula, "Group Homes—New and Differentiated Tools in Child Welfare, Delinquency and Mental Health," CHILD WELFARE, September 1964, 393-397.

(2) Harriet Goldstein, "The Role of a Director in a Group Home," CHILD WELFARE, November 1966, 501-508.

(3) Joseph L. Taylor, "The Child Welfare Agency as the Extended Family," CHILD WELFARE, February 1972, 74-83.

(4) Goldstein, op. cit.

(5) Eva Burmeister, "Living in a Group Home: From 'The Professional Houseparent,' " CHILD WELFARE, March 1960, 24.

(6) Leon Eisenberg, "The Challenge of Change," CHILD WELFARE, April 1960, 16.

(7) Jerome L. Singer, "An Appraisal of the Psychosocial Effectiveness of a Group Home Treatment Program for Adolescent Girls," Association for Jewish Children, unpublished.

(8) Goldstein, op. cit.

(9) Rene Spitz, "Hospitalism," THE PSYCHOANALYTIC STUDY OF THE CHILD, Vol. I. New York: International Universities Press, 1945, 53-74.

(10) John Bowlby, "Grief and Mourning in Infancy and Early Childhood," THE PSYCHOANALYTIC STUDY OF THE CHILD, Vol. XV. New York: International Universities Press, 1960, 9-52.

(11) Anna Freud and Joseph Goldstein, BEYOND THE BEST INTERESTS OF THE CHILD. New York: Free Press, 1973.

(12) Calvin Settlage and Manuel Furer, "Individuation in Separation," JOURNAL OF THE ACADEMY OF CHILD PSYCHIATRY, April 1970, 203-215.

(13) Goldstein, op. cit.

(14) M. E. Allerhand, R. E. Weber and M. Haug; ADAPTATION AND ADAPTABILITY: THE BELLEFAIRE FOLLOWUP STUDY. New York: Child Welfare League of America, 1966.

(15) Goldstein, op. cit.

(16) Morris F. Mayer, "The Group in Residential Treatment of Adolescents," CHILD WELFARE, October 1972, 486.
(17) Z. Alexander Aarons, "Normality and Abnormality in Adolescents," THE PSYCHOANALYTIC STUDY OF THE CHILD, Vol. 25. New York: International Universities Press, 1970, 309-339.
(18) Taylor, op. cit.
(19) Vaira Rozentals, Aaron C. Piper and Hugh Wipple, "Professionalizing the Child Care Worker," CHILD WELFARE, November 1974, 564.
(20) Howard W. Polsky and Daniel S. Claster, THE DYNAMICS OF RESIDENTIAL TREATMENT: A SOCIAL SYSTEM ANALYSIS. Chapel Hill, N.C.: University of North Carolina Press, 1968.
(21) James F. Berwald, "Cottage Parents in a Treatment Institution," CHILD WELFARE, December 1960, 7.
(22) Gisela Konopka, "What House Parents Should Know," CHILDREN, March-April 1956, 54.
(23) Joseph L. Taylor, "The Auspices of Psychotherapy for Children in a Foster Family Care Agency," CHILD WELFARE, May 1962, 207-211.
(24) Seymour S. Kety and David Rosenthal, "Mental Illness in the Adoptive Families of Adopted Schizophrenics," AMERICAN JOURNAL OF PSYCHIATRY, V, 143, September 1971, 307-311.
(25) Joseph J. Schildkraut, "The Catecholamine Hypothesis of Affective Disorders: A Review of the Supporting Evidence," AMERICAN JOURNAL OF PSYCHIATRY, V, 122, 1965, 509-522.
(26) Alvin R. Lucas et al., "Biological Studies in Childhood Schizophrenia," JOURNAL OF AUTISM AND CHILDHOOD SCHIZOPHRENIA, V, 1, 1971, 72-81.
(27) Michael Rutter, "The Influence of Organic and Emotional Factors on the Origin and Outcome of Childhood Psychosis," DEVELOPMENTAL MEDICINE AND CHILD NEUROLOGY, V, 7, 1965, 518-528.
(28) Martin De Jong, EXPERIMENTAL CATATONIA. Baltimore: Williams and Wilkins, 1945.
(29) Seymour S. Kety, David Rosenthal and Paul Wender. "The Types and Prevalence of Schizophrenics," in TRANSMISSION OF SCHIZOPHRENIA, edited by Rosenthal and Kety. Elmsford, N.Y.: Pergamon Press, 1968.
(30) Franz Kallman, HEREDITY IN HEALTH AND MENTAL DISORDER: PRINCIPLES OF PSYCHIATRIC GENETICS IN THE LIGHT OF COMPARATIVE TWIN STUDIES. New York: W. W. Norton, 1953.
(31) Alice Cornelison and Frantz Lidtz, SCHIZOPHRENIA AND THE FAMILY. New York: International Universities Press, 1965.
(32) Loretta Bender, "The Life Course of Schizophrenic Children," JOURNAL OF BIOLOGICAL PSYCHOLOGY, V. 2, 1972, 165-172.

(33) Richard D. Laing and David Cooper, REASON AND VIO-LENCE. New York: Pantheon, 1971.

(34) Joseph L. Taylor, "Remedial Education of Children in Foster Care," CHILD WELFARE, February 1973, 123-128.

(35) Harriet Goldstein, SOCIAL WORK PRACTICE 1966. New York: Columbia University Press, 1966.

(36) Morris F. Mayer, "The Group in Residential Treatment of Adolescents," CHILD WELFARE, October 1972, 487.

(37) Bennet R. Wong, "The Adolescent in Our Changing Society," CHILD WELFARE, July 1968, 412.

(38) Norman Herstein, "The Challenge of Evaluation in Residential Treatment," CHILD WELFARE, March 1975, 141-152.

(39) Julian Meltzoff and Melvin Kornreich, RESEARCH IN PSYCHOTHERAPY. New York: Academic Press, 1970.

(40) Susan Salasin, "Experimentation Revisited: A Conversation With Donald T. Campbell," EVALUATION, I, 3, 1973.

(41) Elaine M. Kasowski, A FOLLOWUP APPRAISAL OF PROCESSES AND CHANGE IN A GROUP HOME PROGRAM FOR DISTURBED ADOLESCENT GIRLS, unpublished doctoral dissertation. City University of New York: 1976.

(42) Herstein, op. cit.

(43) Herstein, op. cit.

(44) Ann W. Shyne, "Evaluation in Child Welfare," CHILD WELFARE, January 1976, 11.

(45) David G. Gil, "Developing Routine Followup Procedures for Child Welfare Services," CHILD WELFARE, May 1964, 229-240.

(46) David Fanshel, "Research in Child Welfare: A Critical Analysis," CHILD WELFARE, December 1962, 484-507.

(47) Kasowski, op. cit.

(48) Morris F. Mayer, Leon H. Richman and Edwin A. Balcerzak, "Residential Group Care for Dependent, Neglected and Emotionally Disturbed Children in the United States and Canada," unpublished.

(49) Henry W. Maier, "Learning to Learn and Living to Live in Residential Treatment," CHILD WELFARE, June 1975, 407.

The Scoring Manual and Scales

I. **Description of Scales** (See Appendix A for scales)

1. There are five scales as follows: 1) Job or School Adequacy; 2) Adjustment to General Daily Living; 3) Peer Relationships— Female; 4) Peer Relationships—Male; and 5) Self-Attitude.

2. Each scale has 11 steps with illustrative profiles depicting each odd-numbered step.

3. Step 11 illustrates "excellent adjustment"; Step 9, "good adjustment"; Step 7, "average adjustment"; Step 5, "Some adjustment"; Step 3, "slight adjustment"; and Step 1, "no adjustment."

4. Graded adjective or adverb phrases are often used within the text of the illustrative profiles to differentiate steps in the scale. (For example, "frequently," "usually," "more often than not," "as often as not," "less often than not," "almost never.")

5. Each scale is made up of two or three weighted dimensions. Judges must consider these relative weights when assigning ratings. (The dimensions and their relative weights are discussed in detail in section V.)

II. **Material to Which Scales Are to Be Applied**

1. *Case Report:* Each case report is made up of three subsidiary reports concerning a specific client (when available, additional information is included). These include a social worker's narrative, a psychological summary and psychiatric interview summary. The entire case report is about 11 single-spaced pages.

III. **Current and Predictive Ratings**

Judges will make three types of ratings: a current rating and two predictive ratings, one with and the other without therapeutic intervention.

1. *Current Intake Ratings:* On the basis of information contained in the case report, judges are to rate the current status of the client on the five scales.

2. *Predictive Ratings:* Based on their professional knowledge

and experience with similar cases, judges will predict the growth potential of individual clients in the five areas surveyed by the scales. More specifically, judges will answer the question, "Given the psychological and situational factors described, where would I expect this client to be on this scale 4 years from now (the actual length of time for which predictions will be made may vary somewhat but will average about 4 years)?" (a) In making the first predictions judges should assume that there has been *no therapeutic intervention* of any sort. (b) In making the second predictive rating, judges should view the client as having undergone 2 to 3 years of optimal therapeutic intervention involving a common residential setting, with continuous social casework and some opportunity for psychotherapy.

Whereas the diagnosis a client receives has some prognostic significance, judges will also want to assess other psychological and situational factors in making predictions. A close look should be taken as to the type of disruptive or self-defeating behavior the girl manifests, her social, cognitive and educational status, her family background and her likely situational prospects for the future. As an example, one might predict that a girl with a history of disrupted family, much antisocial activity, slightly below average IQ, minimum education, and no evidence of vocational aptitudes will have less likelihood of attaining the same final level as a girl from an intact, if temporarily disrupted, family who is above average in intelligence, shows good secretarial skills and has had a recent onset of phobias and anxiety.

The importance of situational factors in determining predictions is worth reiterating. Judges should carefully assess what situational possibilities are likely to confront a girl in 2 years and take these into account in making predictions.

IV. Steps for Use of Scales With Case Reports

It is suggested that judges use the following procedure in applying scales to case reports.

1) Read entire report through.

2) During second reading of report, record all facts relevant to specific scales in space provided on work sheet.

3) Considering one variable at a time, locate approximate range of scale that best describes adjustment depicted in report.

4) Carefully read scale profiles in approximate range and decide on specific rating according to guidelines described in sections V and VI.

5) Enter rating in space provided on work sheet.

V. Scale Dimensions

Each scale is made up of two or three weighted dimensions that judges must consider when assigning ratings.

1) *Job or School Adequacy Scale*

This scale includes three basic dimensions: 1) attendance, 2) work habits, and 3) personal motivation, corresponding to paragraphs one, two and three, respectively. Of these dimensions the second and third, that is, work habits and personal motivation, should be given greater weight. Thus, a girl may claim regular attendance at school or work, yet may receive a low rating if her other statements reveal that she is lax in her responsibilities and shows little personal ambition.

2) *Adjustment to General Daily Living Scale*

a) This scale includes two basic dimensions: 1) management of household responsibilities, and 2) relationship with living mates, corresponding to paragraphs one and two of Appendix. Of these two dimensions, the first, management of household responsibilities, should be given greater weight.

b) The fifth sentence of the scale (identified in the Appendix by an asterisk) concerning manner of execution of household chores is especially important and should be given adequate consideration.

3) *Peer Relationships—Female Scale*

a) This scale includes two basic dimensions: 1) extent of interaction with others, and 2) quality of interaction, corresponding approximately to paragraphs one and two, respectively. Of these two dimensions the second, relating to quality of interaction, is to be given greater weight. Thus, judges should not interpret too literally or rely too heavily on words in the scale describing the exact extent of interaction. (For example, "She contacts friends . . . frequently, regularly, moderately often, occasionally, infrequently, almost never." Similarly, "She maintains some friendships, a few friendships, one or two friendships, etc.") In summary, a girl may claim regular contact with a number of friends but may receive a low rating if her other statements reveal that the nature of these relationships is highly superficial, competitive, etc.

b) The last sentence of this scale (identified by an asterisk) relating to quality of interaction is considered especially important and should be given adequate consideration.

4) *Peer Relationships—Male Scale*

a) This scale includes two basic dimensions: 1) attitude toward relationships with males, and 2) quality of actual interaction, corresponding to paragraphs one and two, respectively. In the case of younger girls (16 years or younger) who have developed only platonic or casual relationships with boys, judges may give the two dimensions equal weight. However, in the case of older girls (approximately 17 or older) who might be expected to have begun romantic dating, judges should give emphasis to the second dimension, quality of actual interaction.

b) Judges should not interpret too literally or rely too heavily on words in the scale describing the exact extent of interaction. (For example, "The girl sees her boyfriend . . . frequently, regularly, moderately often, occasionally, etc.") Similarly, the amount of interest a girl shows in establishing relationships with males (for example, "active interest," "considerable interest," "moderate interest," "some interest," etc.) should be evaluated within the context of the actual quality of interaction. A girl can be "boy crazy," yet have highly disturbed relationships with males.

c) The last sentence in this scale (identified by an asterisk) concerning quality of interaction is considered especially important and should be given adequate consideration.

5) *Self-Attitude Scale*

a) This scale has two major dimensions: 1) self-image, and 2) personal care, corresponding to paragraphs one and two, respectively. These dimensions are to be weighted equally.

b) The tenth sentence on this scale (identified by an asterisk) concerning habits harmful to health is especially important and should be given adequate consideration.

VI. Guidelines for Assigning Ratings "5," "6" or "7"

In assigning ratings judges may often find that the middle range of a scale best describes the adjustment depicted in a report. A decision will then have to be made whether to assign a specific rating of "5," "6" or "7." As this is an *extremely important* decision, the following guidelines are provided to assist judges in making reliable ratings.

1) All scales were constructed so that a rating of "7" implies average adjustment. If a girl receives a rating of "5" this means that a judge assesses her adjustment to be somewhat below average in comparison to her peer group. Therefore, as a start, it may be helpful for a judge to ask herself the general question, "Is this girl functioning moderately well in this area or is her functioning somewhat below that which would be expected for a girl of her age?"

2) In section V each scale is discussed in terms of two or three major dimensions and their associated weights. In general, it can be stated that if the heavily weighted dimension falls *solidly* into one rating category and the less heavily weighted dimension falls into an adjacent rating category (e.g., if the heavily weighted dimension is a "5" and the less heavily weighted dimension is a "7," or vice versa), the overall rating should be the same as the rating assigned the more heavily weighted dimension. If, however, the heavily weighted dimension has one or two elements from the same rating category as the less heavily weighted dimension, (e.g., if the heavily weighted dimension is basically a "5" with one or two elements of "7" when the less heavily weighted dimension is "7," or vice versa) the overall rating should be "6."

To illustrate, it was stated earlier that the scale "Adjustment to Living Situation" has two dimensions: 1) management of household responsibilities, and 2) relationship with living mates. The first dimension, management of household responsibilities, was more heavily weighted. As an example of a specific case, a judge may evaluate a girl as a "5" on management of household responsibilities and a "7" on relationship with living mates. Since the former is the more heavily weighted dimension, the overall rating would be "5." However, if a judge felt a girl was basically a "5" on household responsibilities, but had some elements of "7" on this dimension, and if she was a "7" on relationships with living mates, the judge should assign the rating of "6."

(Where there is a greater difference than two scale steps between the scores a girl earns on two dimensions, the overall score should be closer to the score earned on the more heavily weighted dimension. For example, a girl might claim she has a good relationship with her roommate ("8"), but might further indicate that she and her roommate are content to neglect household chores, live in unkempt surroundings, etc. ("3"). In this case a judge might assign an overall rating of "4." It should be noted, however, that such extreme differences between dimension scores will occur only rarely.)

Because of the existence of weighted dimensions, judges cannot assign ratings by simply counting the number of sentences in profile 7 that best fit a specific client and compare them with the number of best fitting sentences in profile 5. Instead, it is important that judges be familiar with the dimensions and their associated weights and on this basis assign ratings.

Note: The rating of "6" should be used sparingly and in accordance with the foregoing guidelines.

VII. Location of Relevant Passages in Case Reports for Making Specific Ratings

Information relevant to specific scales may be found at any place in the case report. For this reason it was suggested that each report receive two thorough readings.

In addition to such important random sentences, there are specific passages or paragraphs in the case report relevant to specific scales. The placement of these passages is briefly outlined in the following:

1) *Case Report*

a) Job or School Adequacy—Section III in social worker's narrative under heading "School Adjustment"; psychologist's assessment of intellectual functioning, especially results of IQ and Wide Range Achievement Test; comments throughout report.

b) Adjustment to General Daily Living—Section III of social worker's narrative under heading "Relationship to Parents and Family"; comments throughout report.

c) Peer Relationships—Female—Section III in social worker's narrative under heading "Child's Personality," also heading "Social Relationships"; psychologist's statements concerning effectiveness in social situations; comments throughout report.

d) Peer Relationships—Male—Section III in social worker's narrative under heading "Child's Personality"; also heading "Social Relationships"; psychologist's statements about sex-role identification and attitudes toward men; comments throughout report.

e) Self-Attitude—Section III in social worker's narrative under heading "Child's Personality"; psychologist's statements concerning self-image; psychiatrist's impressions; comments throughout report.

To reiterate, judges should be thoroughly familiar with the entire case report before assigning specific ratings. Information gleaned from passages *not listed* in the foregoing is often crucial in determining ratings.

APPENDIX A

JOB OR SCHOOL ADEQUACY

11. Excellent Adjustment

Attends school or work very regularly and consistently. Rarely absent without a sound reason.

Very dependable and consistent worker. Sets goals and strives to attain them by following a self-imposed schedule of activities. Almost always perseveres in tasks and is not easily distracted.

When frustrated, almost always strives to overcome obstacles and succeed. Shows a high degree of imagination and inventiveness in job or schoolwork. Indicates that work is a source of considerable satisfaction to her.

Shows marked drive, ambition and desire for personal achievement. Has rarely changed jobs or schools, and when this has occurred it has been due to necessity (e.g., moving to a distant neighborhood) or for advancement. Sees her present efforts as definitely relevant to her future.

9. Good Adjustment

Has a fairly regular attendance record at school or work, with less than the usual amount of absenteeism. Is infrequently absent without a sound reason.

Usually a dependable worker. Usually sets goals and strives to attain them by following a self-imposed schedule of goal-directed activities. Usually perseveres in tasks and can usually resist distraction. In the event of failure or frustration, usually strives to overcome obstacles and succeed. Shows a considerable degree of imagination and inventiveness in job or schoolwork. Indicates that her work is usually a source of satisfaction to her.

Displays considerable drive, ambition and desire for personal achievement. Has changed jobs or school infrequently. When this has occurred it has usually been due to practical necessity or for advancement. Sees her present efforts as relevant to her future.

7. Average Adjustment

Has a fairly regular attendance record at school or work, with no more than the usual amount of absenteeism. On infrequent occasions is absent for unsound or not clearly understood reasons.

At times, is a conscientious worker; at other times seems to hold back and be slack in her responsibilities. Sometimes sets goals and strives to attain them. As often as not, follows a schedule of goal-directed activities, whether this schedule be self-imposed or externally directed. Is capable of persevering in tasks but can be distracted. In the event of failure or frustration, shows some evidence of striving to overcome obstacles and succeed. Shows a moderate degree of imagination and inventiveness in her job or school work. Indicates that she derives a fair degree of satisfaction from her work.

Displays a moderate amount of drive, ambition and desire for personal achievement. Has changed jobs or schools no more than average. May not have shown much notable advancement. Sees her present efforts as somewhat related to her future.

5. Some Adjustment

Has a fairly regular attendance record at school or work, yet there is more than the usual amount of absenteeism. At times, is absent for unsound or not clearly understood reasons.

Is a somewhat inconsistent worker who sometimes tries to expend effort, but cannot sustain it unless she has direction. Usually does not set goals. Only occasionally will follow a schedule of goal-directed activities, but the schedule is more often externally directed than self-imposed, and not adhered to with any degree of regularity. Is somewhat distractable and does not persevere too well in tasks. In the event of failure or frustration, tends to give up or react emotionally rather than try to overcome the obstacles. Usually relies on the work and example of others rather than on her own creative flair, although she may show occasional ingenuity. Indicates variation in her satisfaction with her job or schoolwork; at times, she is pleased, at other times displeased.

Displays some drive, ambition and desire for personal achievement. May have changed jobs or school more frequently than average. At times, moved from a higher to slightly lower position or school program (for example, from an academic to commercial course). Sees her present efforts as slightly related to her future.

3. Slight Adjustment

Has an irregular school or work attendance record. May be absent for periods of time, usually with unsound or not clearly understood reasons.

Is rarely a dependable worker. Seldom sets goals or tries to attain these goals. Will rarely follow a schedule of goal-directed activities, even if it is structured for her. Shows little perseverance in tasks and is easily distracted. Usually gives up or reacts emotionally in the face of failure or frustration, and makes little effort to overcome obstacles. Shows little imagination and inventiveness in her job or schoolwork. Indicates that she usually finds her work distasteful and dissatisfying.

Displays very little drive, ambition or desire for personal achievement. Has had frequent job or school changes. (May have failed in school or may have been dismissed by employers.) Sees present efforts as minimally related to her future.

1. No Adjustment

Has a highly irregular school or work attendance record. At intervals may be absent for extended periods of time with unsound or not clearly understood reasons.

On the occasions when she does attend, is very undependable and shows no sense of responsibility. Will hardly ever follow a schedule of goal-directed activities even if it is structured for her. Shows practically no perseverance in tasks and is very easily distracted and unable to attend. In the face of failure or frustration, almost always gives up or reacts emotionally, and makes no constructive attempts to overcome obstacles. Shows very little imagination or inventiveness in her work. Indicates that she finds work very distasteful and dissatisfying.

Shows no drive, ambition or desire for personal achievement. Tried a number of jobs or schools unsuccessfully. Does not see work as relevant to her future.

ADJUSTMENT TO GENERAL DAILY LIVING

11. Excellent Adjustment

Has achieved an excellent adjustment in her living situation. Is an active participant in ongoing household activities. In personal habits, such as eating, sleeping and bathing, behavior is congruent with household standards and fits into an orderly routine of such activities at home. Keeps her living quarters attractive, clean and orderly. Willingly takes responsibility for household chores(°). (For a younger girl, this would include keeping her room clean and neat and doing other regularly assigned tasks. For an older, married girl this would include full household responsibilities, including cooking, shopping, house cleaning, laundering, etc. An older, single girl would be expected to fulfill these same duties or to cooperate in sharing them with a roommate.) Often makes an extra effort to do a special job (e.g., redecorate her room, prepare a special dish, etc.)

Shows an awareness of the needs of her living mates and does not infringe upon their rights. Seeks out the company of living mates and regularly engages in mutually satisfying conversations and activities with them.

9. Good Adjustment

Has achieved a good adjustment in her living situation. Most of the time is an active participant in ongoing household activities. In personal habits, such as eating, sleeping and bathing, behavior is congruent with household standards, although she occasionally experiences difficulty in following a routine. Most of the time keeps her living quarters attractive, clean and orderly. Occasionally complains, but usually takes responsibility for household chores (*).

Is usually considerate of the needs of her living mates and only occasionally infringes on their rights. Most often seeks out the company of living mates and is able to engage in mutually satisfying conversations with them.

7. Average Adjustment

Has made a moderate adjustment to her living situation. More often than not is a willing participant in ongoing household activities. Maintains proper eating, sleeping and bathing habits (also for her family, if she is married), but experiences some difficulty in following a routine. (For example, a younger girl may sometimes prefer to eat alone at odd hours.) Makes some attempt to decorate her living quarters and keep them fairly neat and orderly. Sometimes complains, but more often than not takes responsibility for household chores (*).

Is moderately considerate of her living mates, although she sometimes infringes upon their rights. Seeks moderate contact with her living mates and is sometimes able to engage in mutually satisfying conversations with them.

5. Some Adjustment

Has made some adjustment to her living situation. As often as not, is a willing participant in ongoing household activities. For the most part maintains proper eating, sleeping and bathing habits (also for her family, if she is married), although she has considerable difficulty following a routine. Makes some attempt to decorate her living quarters, but they usually have an untidy appearance. As often as not, takes responsibility for household chores, although she may perform them in a superficial, cursory manner (*). (For example, a younger girl might superficially clean her room every few weeks. An older, married girl might meet her family's needs with a minimum effort, that is, serve TV dinners, launder only when she has no more clean outfits, etc.)

Shows some consideration for her living mates, but as often as not, infringes on their rights. (For example, she does not clean up after herself, monopolizes the phone, fails to inform living mates when she intends to be away from home and approximately when she will return, etc.) Seeks some contact with her living mates and is occasionally able to engage in conversations with them.

3. Slight Adjustment

Has made a slight adjustment to her living situation. Most often is unwilling to participate in ongoing household activities. Experiences considerable difficulty in maintaining proper eating, sleeping and bathing habits (also for her family, if she is married) or in following a routine in these areas. Makes infrequent attempts to decorate her living quarters, which usually have a disordered appearance. More often than not neglects household chores or performs them in a highly superficial, cursory manner (*).

Shows slight consideration for her living mates and more often than not infringes on their rights. Only occasionally seeks contact with her living mates and engages in conversations with them.

1. No Adjustment

Has made no adjustment to her living situation. Is almost always unwilling to participate in ongoing household activities. Makes no effort to maintain proper eating, sleeping and bathing habits (also for her family, if she is married) or to follow a routine in these areas. Takes no interest in decorating her living quarters, which almost always have a disordered appearance. Almost always neglects household chores (*).

Shows very little consideration for her living mates and usually infringes upon their rights. Rarely seeks contact with her living mates and usually avoids conversations with them.

PEER RELATIONSHIPS—FEMALE

11. Excellent Adjustment

Shows an active interest in her peers. Seeks out friends and is very responsive to the overtures of others. Makes friends readily and can maintain these friendships over an extended period of time. Has girl friends whom she contacts frequently.

Is able to develop and share personal and organizational interests with friends. Indicates that her relationships with other girls are enjoyable and mutually helpful, with a great deal of sharing and understanding (*).

9. Good Adjustment

Shows a considerable interest in her peers. Initiates interactions regularly and readily responds to the overtures of others. Manages to make friends and to maintain these friendships over a considerable period of time. Has girl friends whom she contacts regularly.

Is usually able to develop and share personal and organizational interests with friends. Indicates that her relationships with other girls are usually enjoyable and mutually helpful, with considerable sharing and understanding (*).

7. Average Adjustment

Shows a moderate interest in her peers. More often than not initiates interactions and responds to the overtures of others. Occasionally has difficulty in making friends, but can maintain some friendships over a moderate period of time. Has girl friends whom she contacts moderately often.

Develops and shares organizational interests with acquaintances, and can also share some personal interests with friends. Indicates that more often than not her relationships with other girls are moderately enjoyable and mutually helpful, with some sharing and understanding (*).

5. Some Adjustment

Shows some interest in her peers. As often as not initiates interactions and responds to the overtures of others. Has some difficulty in making friends, but can maintain a few friendships over some period of time. Contacts her friends somewhat occasionally.

Uses the formal structure of an organization to develop and share organizational interests with acquaintances. Can also share a few personal interests with friends. Indicates that the nature of her relationships with other girls is variable; at times she finds their company enjoyable and mutually helpful, at other times she may react in a somewhat competitive or negative manner or may withdraw (*).

3. Slight Adjustment

Has a slight interest in her peers. Most often, fails to initiate interactions and only occasionally responds to the overtures of others. Has considerable difficulty in making friends, but can maintain one or two friendships or acquaintanceships for short periods of time. Has infrequent contact with her friends or acquaintances.

Most often uses the formal structure of an organization to develop and share organizational interests with acquaintances. Is only rarely able to share personal interests with friends. Indicates that she rarely finds relationships with other girls enjoyable or mutually helpful. Most often, either reacts in an unduly competitive or negative manner or withdraws (*).

1. No Adjustment

Has no interest in her peers. Does not initiate interactions and avoids overtures of others. Is unable to maintain contact with peers for any period of time. Has almost no friends or casual acquaintances.

Is usually unable to use the framework of a formal organization to develop friendships or acquaintanceships, and cannot share personal interests with others. Indicates that she almost never finds relationships with other girls enjoyable or mutually helpful. Typically reacts in a highly competitive or negative manner, or remains distant and withdrawn (*).

PEER RELATIONSHIPS—MALE

11. Excellent Adjustment

Shows an active interest in establishing and maintaining relationships with male peers. Seeks out the company of boys similar in age to herself by attending parties, social clubs, etc.

Has a differentiated perception of male peers and is able to relate to them as individuals. Makes friends and can maintain these friendships.

The girl may have a boyfriend or may enjoy platonic relationships with boys she sees frequently. (Although able to relate to many men, the young woman has a boyfriend or husband with whom she has been able to enjoy a special relationship over an extended period of time.) Is able to develop and share personal and organizational interests with her boyfriend. Is compatible with her boyfriend both educationally and intellectually. Indicates that her relationships with male peers are highly satisfying, with a great deal of mutual affection, respect and understanding (*).

9. Good Adjustment

Shows a considerable interest in establishing and maintaining relationships with male peers. Is often receptive to invitations to attend parties, social clubs, etc., where she might meet boys similar in age to herself. For the most part, has a differentiated perception of men and is able to relate to them as individuals. Manages to make friends with male peers and to maintain these friendships.

The girl may have a boyfriend or may enjoy casual relationships with boys she sees regularly. (The young woman has a boyfriend or husband with whom she has been able to enjoy a special relationship over a considerable period of time.) Is usually able to develop and share organizational and personal interests with her boyfriend. For the most part, is compatible with her boyfriend both educationally and intellectually. Indicates that her relationships with male peers are satisfying, with a considerable degree of mutual affection, respect and understanding (*).

7. Average Adjustment

Shows a moderate interest in establishing and maintaining relationships with male peers. Is sometimes receptive to invitations to attend parties, social clubs, etc., where she might meet males similar in age to herself. Has a moderately differentiated perception of male peers and is usually able to relate to them as individuals. Has some difficulty in making friends, but can maintain some friendships over a moderate period of time.

The girl may have a boyfriend or may enjoy casual relationships with boys she sees moderately often. (The young woman has had long-term relationships with boyfriends or a husband.) More often than not, is able to develop and share organizational and personal interests with her boyfriend. Although, for the most part she is compatible with her boyfriend, some slight differences in education or intellectual ability may exist. Indicates that her relationships with male peers are most often moderately satisfying, with an adequate degree of mutual affection, respect and understanding (*). However, on occasion may react in a slightly aggressive or sexual manner or may withdraw (*). (For example, a slightly aggressive pattern may be shown by a girl who is mildly critical of her boyfriend, leading to occasional arguments and disagreements. A slightly withdrawn pattern may be shown by a girl who occasionally experiences difficulty accepting warmth or closeness from her boyfriend.)

5. Some Adjustment

Shows some interest in establishing and maintaining relationships with male peers. Is occasionally receptive to invitations to attend parties, social clubs, etc., where she might meet boys similar in age to herself. Has a somewhat differentiated perception of male peers, although at times she tends to stereotype them. (For example, she may tend to view men as excessively domineering, primarily interested in sex, etc.) Has some difficulty making friends, but can maintain some friendships for some period of time.

The girl may have a boyfriend or casual relationships with boys she sees occasionally. (The young woman has had some long-term relationships with boyfriends or a husband.) Is able to develop and share some organizational and personal interests with her boyfriend. Although she is compatible with her boyfriend in some areas, significant differences in education or intellectual ability may exist. Indicates that the nature of her relationships with male peers is variable; at times experiences some satisfactions, with some mutual affection, respect and understanding; at other times may react in an unduly aggressive or sexual manner, or may withdraw (*). (For example, an unduly aggressive pattern might be shown by a girl who is considerably critical of her boyfriend, leading to arguments and disagreements that are not readily resolved. An unduly withdrawn pattern might be shown by a girl who has some difficulty tolerating closeness from a male and who may remain superficially committed to the relationship. She may explain this lack of commitment by finding fault with her boyfriend and expressing unrealistically high standards for what she is seeking in a man. Alternatively, the girl's complaints may appear justified, although she repeatedly becomes associated with men of the same type.)

3. Slight Adjustment

Has a slight interest in establishing and maintaining relationships with male peers. Rarely attends parties, social clubs, etc., where she might meet boys similar in age to herself. Has a slightly differentiated perception of male peers and often tends to stereotype them in a negative manner. Has considerable difficulty making friends and can maintain contact for relatively short periods of time.

Where she has been able to form a relationship, the couple are able to share only a narrow range of organizational and personal interests. Considerable differences in education or intellectual ability may exist. Indicates that the nature of her relationships with male peers is quite variable; at times she experiences slight satisfactions; however, she most often interacts in a highly aggressive or sexual manner or withdraws (*). (For example, a highly aggressive pattern would be shown by a girl who continually criticizes her boyfriend, leading to numerous arguments and disagreements that are rarely resolved and that threaten the relationship. A highly withdrawn pattern might be shown by a girl who has considerable difficulty tolerating closeness from a male and who participates in short-lived, superficial relationships.)

1. No Adjustment

Has almost no interest in establishing and maintaining relationships with male peers. Usually avoids all parties, social clubs, etc., where she might meet boys similar in age to herself. Has a negative and undifferentiated perception of male peers and almost always stereotypes them. Is unable to maintain contact with individual boys for any period of time, but may have many indiscriminate, short-lived relationships.

Where she has been able to form a relationship, the couple are able to share only a narrow range of personal or organizational interests. Indicates that relationships with male peers provide only superficial physical satisfactions, with very little mutual affection, respect and understanding. Typically, interacts in a markedly aggressive or sexual manner or may remain distant and withdrawn (*). (For example, a markedly aggressive pattern might be shown by a girl whose interactions with her boyfriend mostly take the form of verbal or physical battles. A markedly sexual pattern might be shown by a girl who has many indiscriminate short-lived contacts in which her primary involvement is sexual. A markedly withdrawn pattern might be shown by a girl who expresses no interest in men and avoids all interaction with them.)

SELF-ATTITUDE

11. Excellent Adjustment
Has a high degree of self-worth. Sees her strengths and weaknesses very realistically. Has high self-acceptance as to own traits, abilities and characteristics. Frequently judges self favorably, as compared with others. Possesses self-confidence as to outcome of her own efforts and her ability to overcome obstacles and solve problems. Very often feels loved, liked, wanted, respected, accepted and understood.

Keeps self in very good physical condition. Shows a decided respect for her body by having regular medical and dental check-ups. Follows recommendations for maintaining good health. Does not engage in habits harmful to health (*) (e.g., excessive eating, smoking, taking of drugs, etc.). Is evidently careful about grooming. Chooses appropriate combinations of clothes, keeps herself clean and neat, and cares for her personal appearance with regularity and thoroughness.

9. Good Adjustment
Has considerable self-worth. For the most part sees strengths and weaknesses realistically. Usually has self-acceptance as to own traits, abilities and characteristics. More often than not judges self favorably, as compared with others. Usually possesses

confidence as to outcome of own efforts and her ability to overcome obstacles and solve problems. More often than not feels loved, liked, wanted, respected, accepted and understood.

Keeps self in good physical condition. Usually has regular medical and dental checkups and follows recommendations for maintaining good health. Usually does not engage in habits harmful to health (*). Is usually careful about grooming. More often than not chooses appropriate combinations of clothes, keeps herself clean and neat, and cares for her personal appearance with regularity and thoroughness.

7. Average Adjustment

Has an adequate degree of self-worth. Has a moderately realistic awareness of her makeup, although sometimes exaggerates her strengths and minimizes limits, or vice versa. Has an adequate degree of self-acceptance as to own traits, abilities and characteristics. As often as not judges self favorably, as compared with others. Possesses a moderate degree of self-confidence as to the outcome of her own efforts, and in her ability to overcome obstacles and solve problems. As often as not feels loved, liked, wanted, respected, accepted and understood.

Generally keeps self in good physical condition. Recognizes the importance of medical and dental checkups, but may sometimes neglect to schedule routine appointments. Although not engaging excessively in habits harmful to health, in one area may sometimes exceed the limits recommended by professionals for maintaining good health (*). (For example, smoking a pack of cigarettes a week, being 10-15 pounds overweight, etc.) Appears moderately well groomed. Is moderately successful in choosing appropriate combinations of clothes, keeping herself clean and neat, and caring for her personal appearance.

5. Some Adjustment

Has some self-worth. Tends to waver between a realistic awareness of her makeup and an unrealistic view. Has some self-acceptance, but as often as not expresses dissatisfaction with own traits, abilities and characteristics. As often as not judges self unfavorably, as compared with others. Has a somewhat lowered degree of self-confidence as to the outcome of her own efforts and in her ability to overcome obstacles and solve problems. Tends toward feelings of being unwanted, unloved, disliked, disrespected, rejected and misunderstood. (Note: Alternatively, a girl may be assigned a rating of "5" if her confidence in herself appears somewhat exaggerated.)

There is some variation in her personal care. Sometimes carries through the recommendations of professionals about caring for herself. At other times neglects to schedule appointments for the treatment of existing conditions. Although she recognizes some practices as detrimental to health, as often as not is unable to prevent herself from engaging excessively in one harmful habit (for example, she may be a chain smoker, may be excessively overweight, etc.) (*). Although she makes some effort to appear well groomed, she is not always successful. There is some variation in her ability to choose appropriate combinations of clothes, keep herself clean and neat and care for her personal appearance.

3. Slight Adjustment

Has a slight feeling of self-worth. Tends toward an unrealistic self-view. Has slight self-acceptance as to own characteristics, traits and abilities. Usually belittles, downgrades and underrates herself. Possesses only a slight degree of self-confidence as to the outcome of own efforts and in ability to overcome obstacles and solve problems. Usually feels unwanted, unloved, disliked, disrespected, rejected and misunderstood. (Note: Alternatively, a girl may be assigned a rating of "3" if her confidence in herself appears considerably exaggerated.)

Tends to neglect physical condition. Rarely schedules routine checkups and tends to ignore existing disorders. Is usually unable to prevent herself from engaging excessively in one or more habits harmful to health (*). Tends to be careless about grooming. There is considerable variation in ability to choose appropriate combinations of clothes, keep herself clean and neat, and care for her personal appearance.

1. No Adjustment

Has marked feelings of personal unworthiness. Is very unrealistic in evaluating her strengths and weaknesses. Has very low self-regard as to characteristics, traits and abilities. Characteristically belittles, downgrades and underrates herself. Possesses a very low degree of self-confidence as to the outcome of own efforts, and is convinced of inability to overcome obstacles and solve problems. Almost always feels unwanted, unloved, disliked, disrespected, rejected and misunderstood. (Note: Alternatively, a girl may be assigned a rating of "1" if her confidence in herself appears highly exaggerated.)

Neglects physical condition. Almost never schedules routine checkups and ignores even serious existing disorders. Rarely follows recommendations for maintaining good health. Makes practically no effort to prevent herself from engaging excessively in harmful and dangerous habits (e.g., drug addiction) (*). Is careless about grooming. Makes almost no effort to choose appropriate combinations of clothes, keep herself clean and neat, and care for her personal appearance.

SCORING SHEET

Client:

1) Job or School Adequacy
Ratings:

————————Current ————————Predictive (without intervention)

————————Predictive (with optimal intervention)

Comments:————————————————————————————

————————————————————————————————————

2) Adjustment to General Daily Living
Ratings:

————————Current ————————Predictive (without intervention)

————————Predictive (with optimal intervention)

Comments: ———————————————————————————

————————————————————————————————————

3) Peer Relations—Female
Ratings:

————————Current ————————Predictive (without intervention)

————————Predictive (with optimal intervention)

Comments:————————————————————————————

————————————————————————————————————

4) Peer Relationships—Male
Ratings:

————Current ————Predictive (without intervention)

————Predictive (with optimal intervention)

Comments:————————————————————

5) Self-Attitude
Ratings:

————Current ————Predictive (without intervention)

————Predictive (with optimal intervention)

Comments:————————————————————

Summary statement:————————————————